BLAST FROM THE PAST

80'S POP ART BY MILLENNIAL ARTIST

JUSTIN VALENTI

Valenti Publications
BLAST FROM THE PAST
80's Pop Art
Maryland, USA
© 2018

Edited by Tawd b. Dorenfeld,
Tink Tank Animate LLC

www.jkvalenti2014.wordpress.com/portfolio

BLAST FROM THE PAST

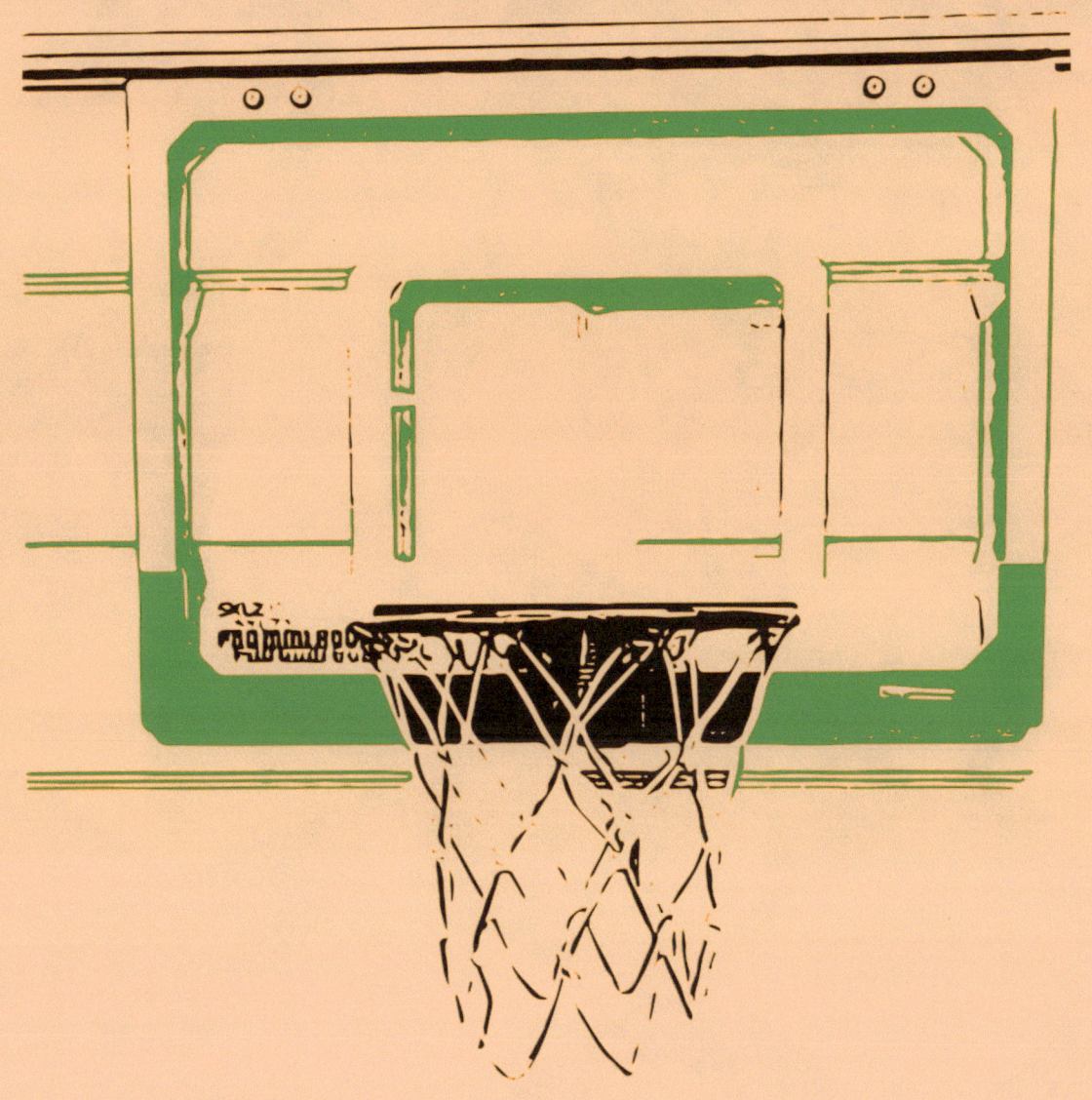

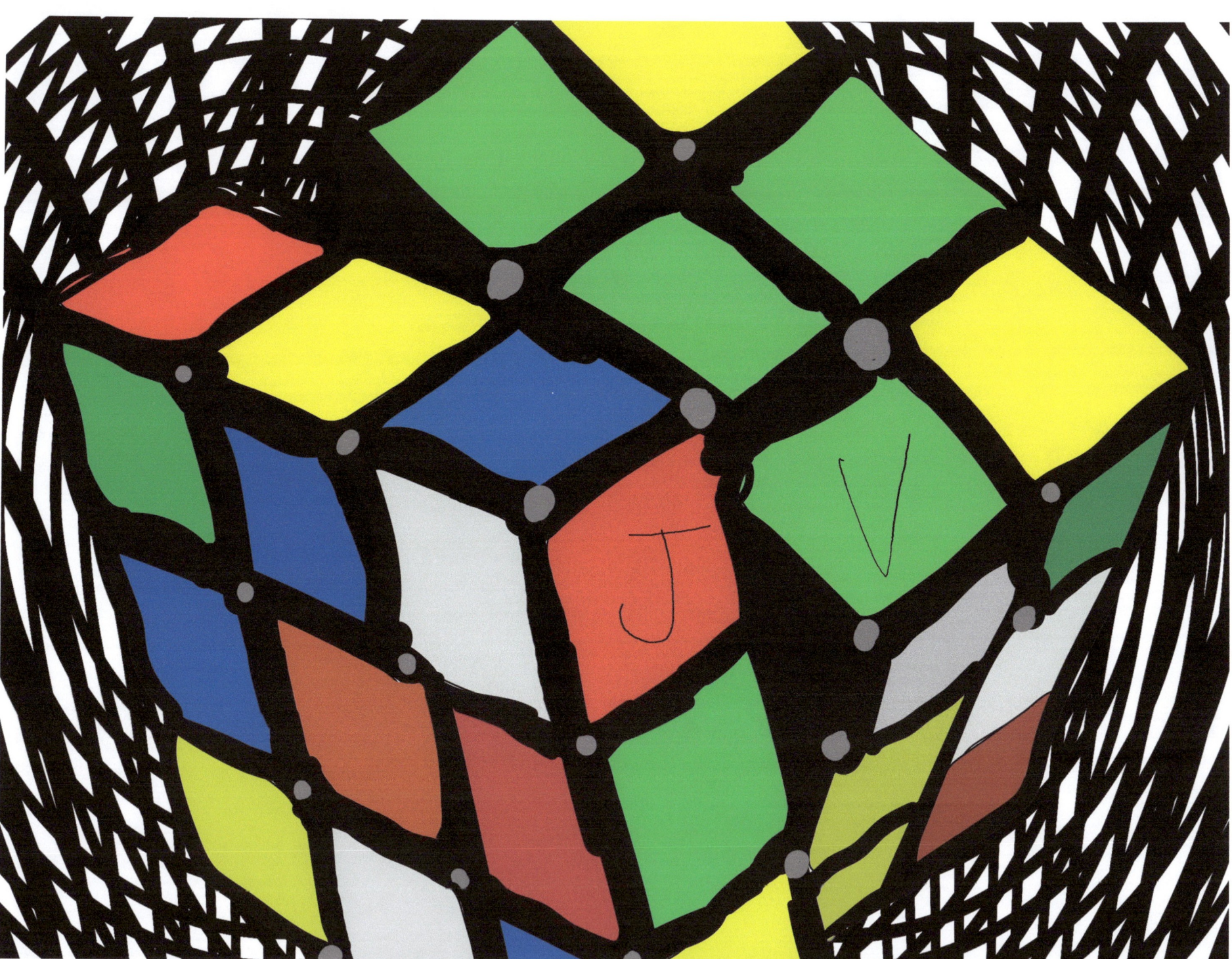

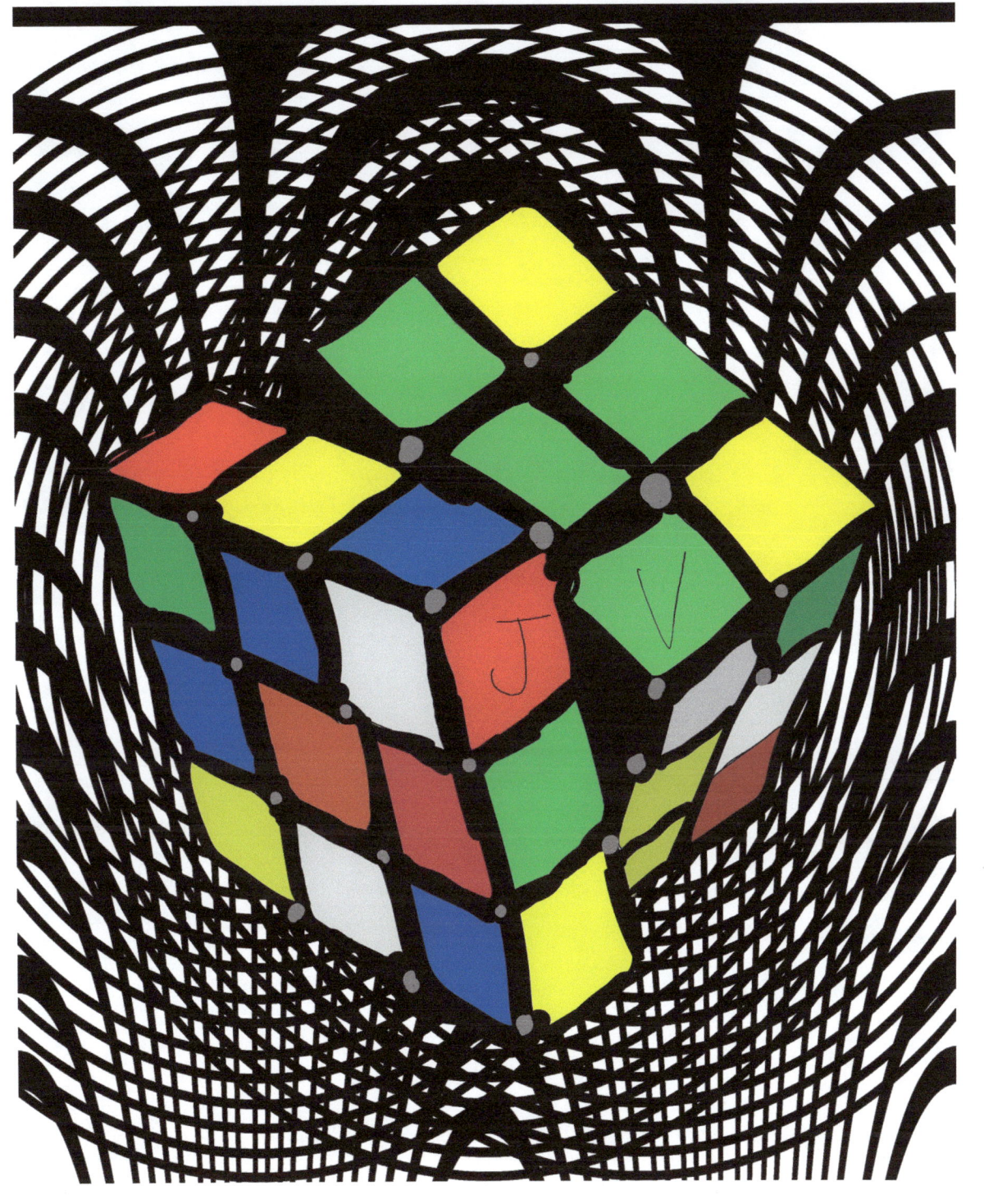

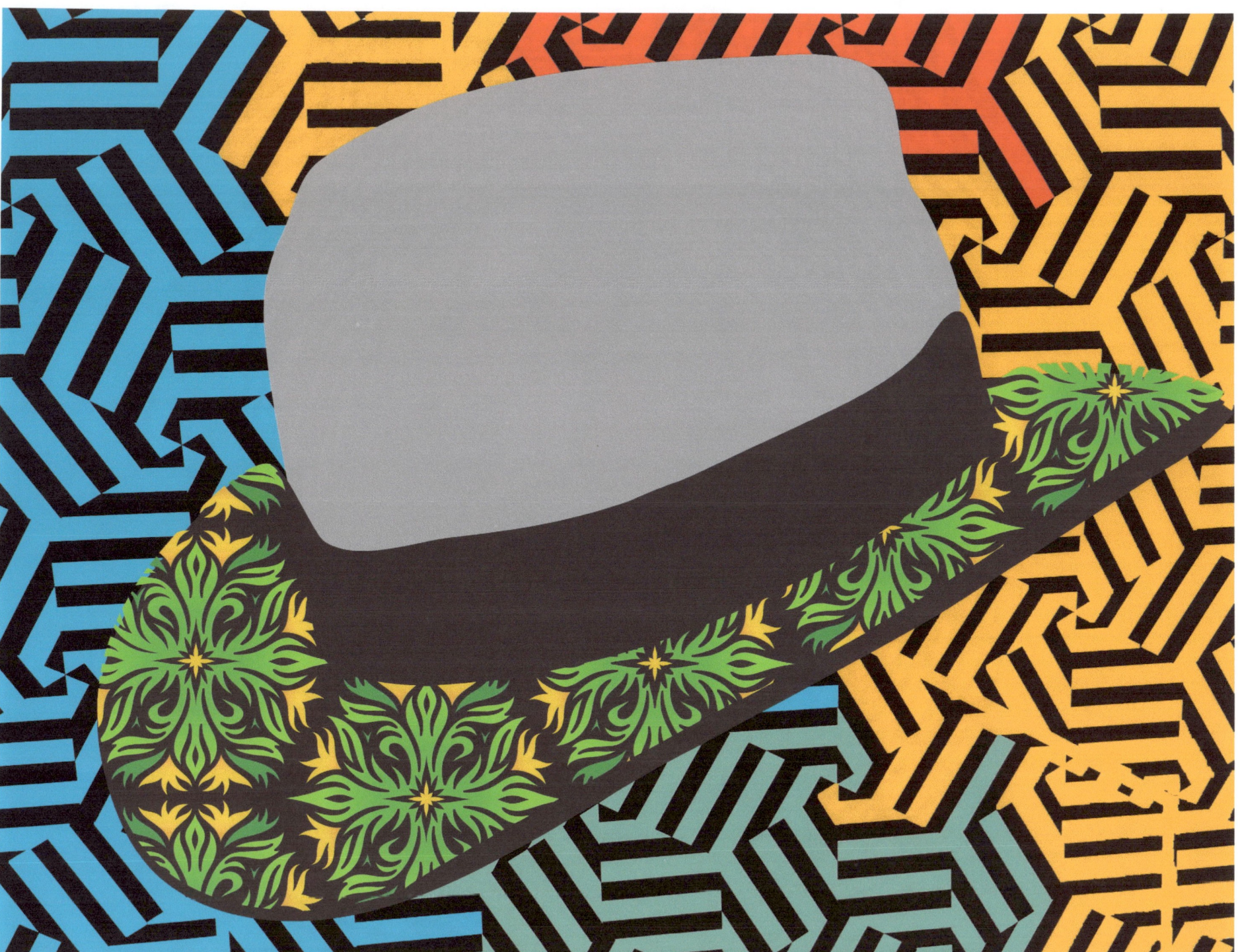

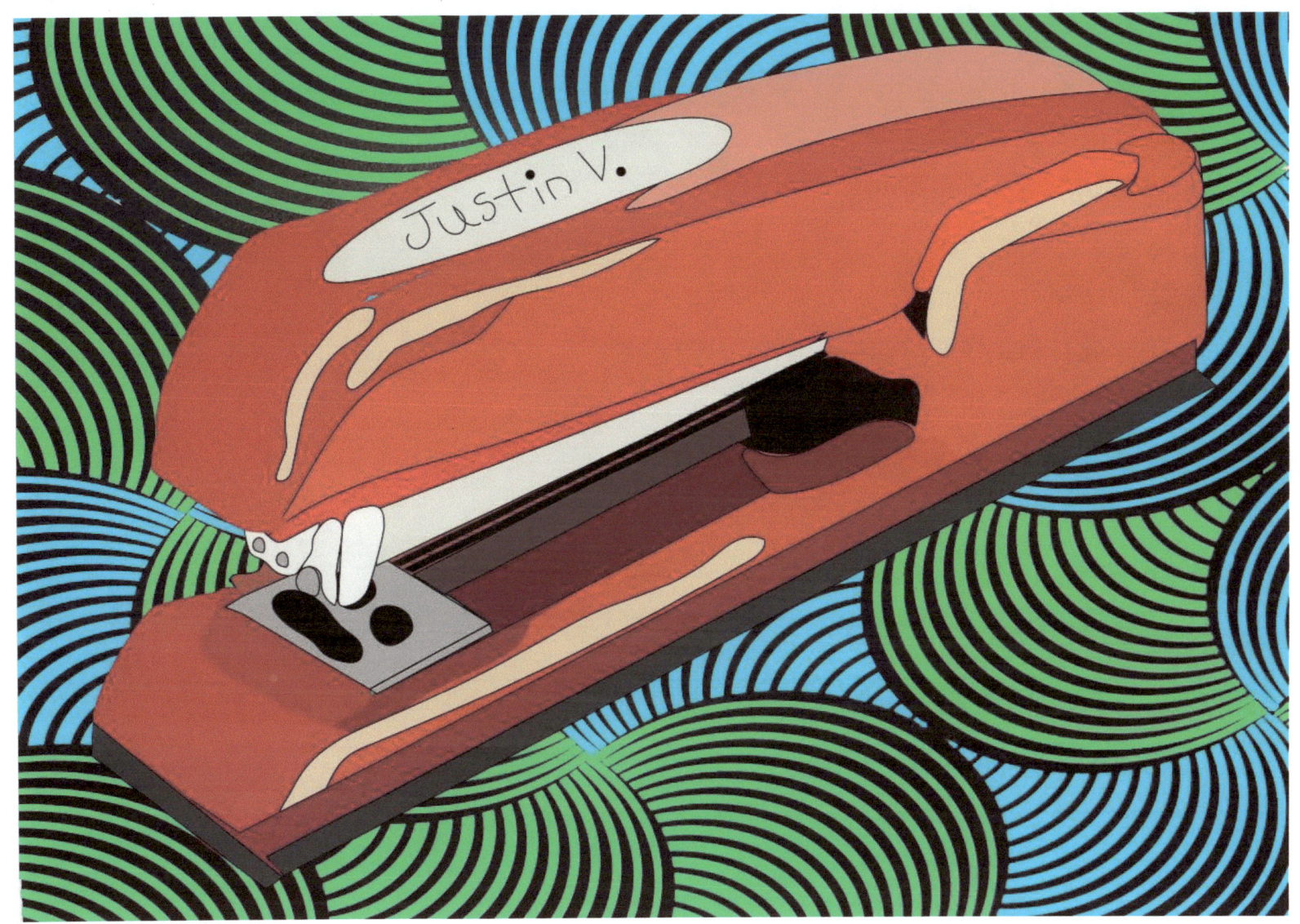

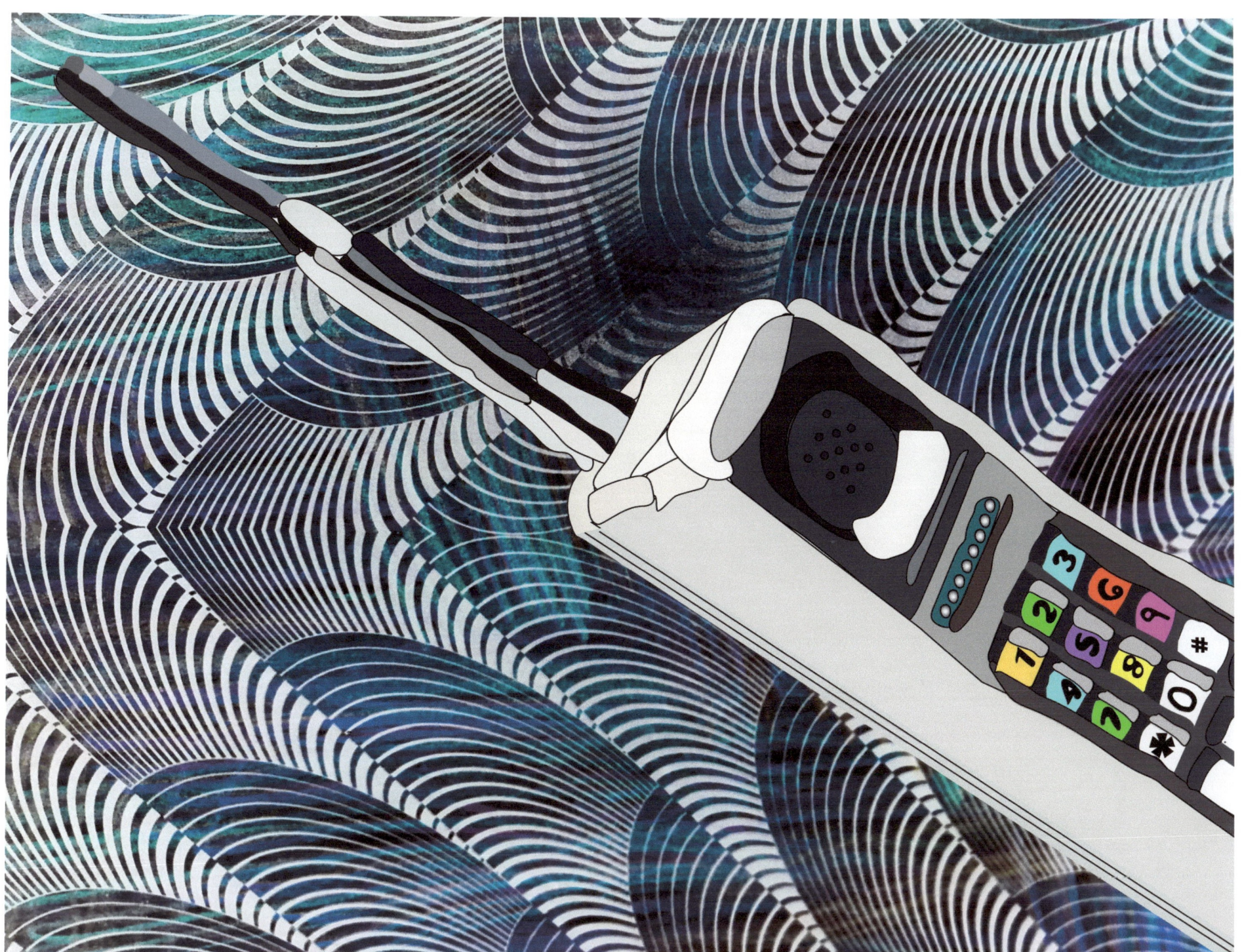

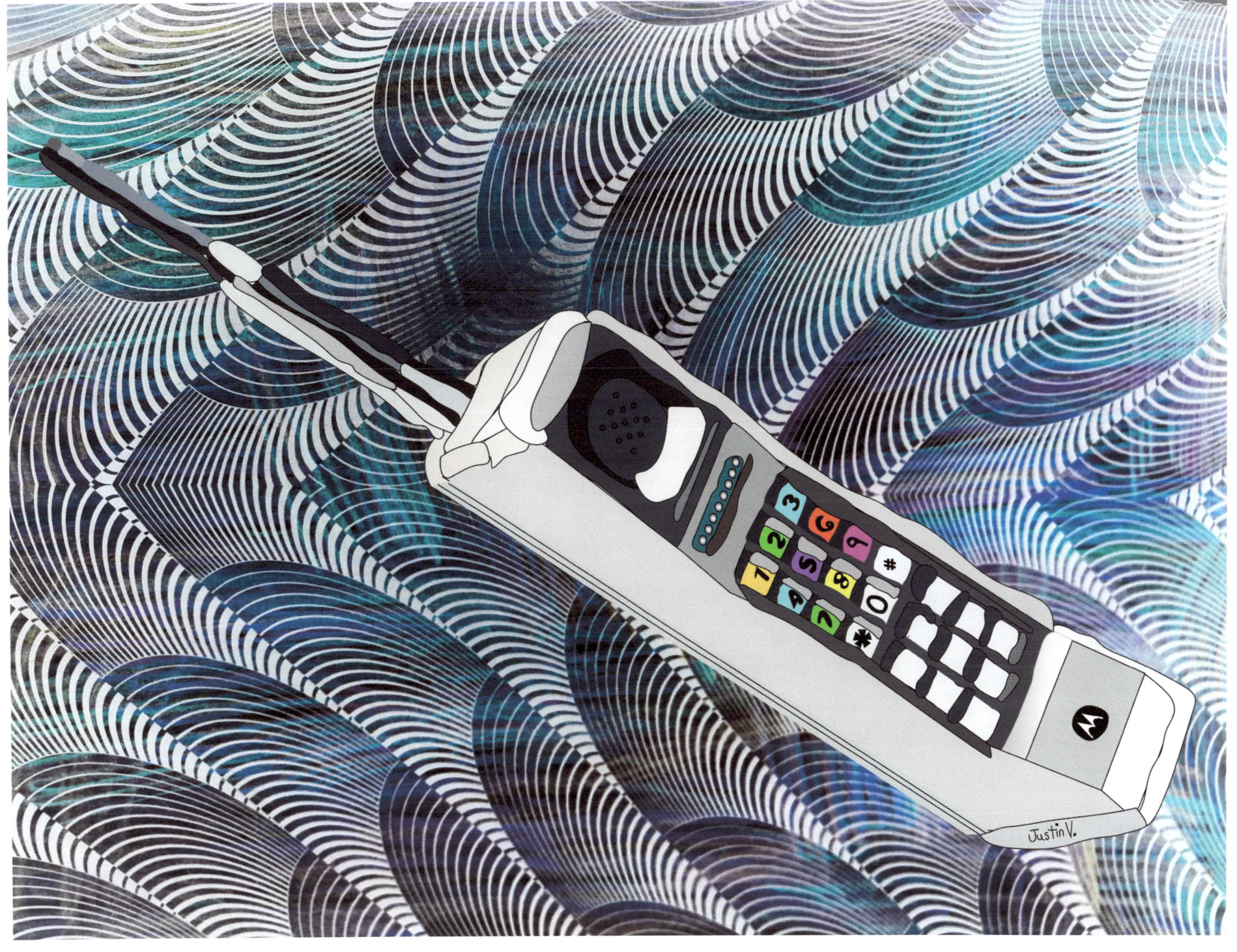

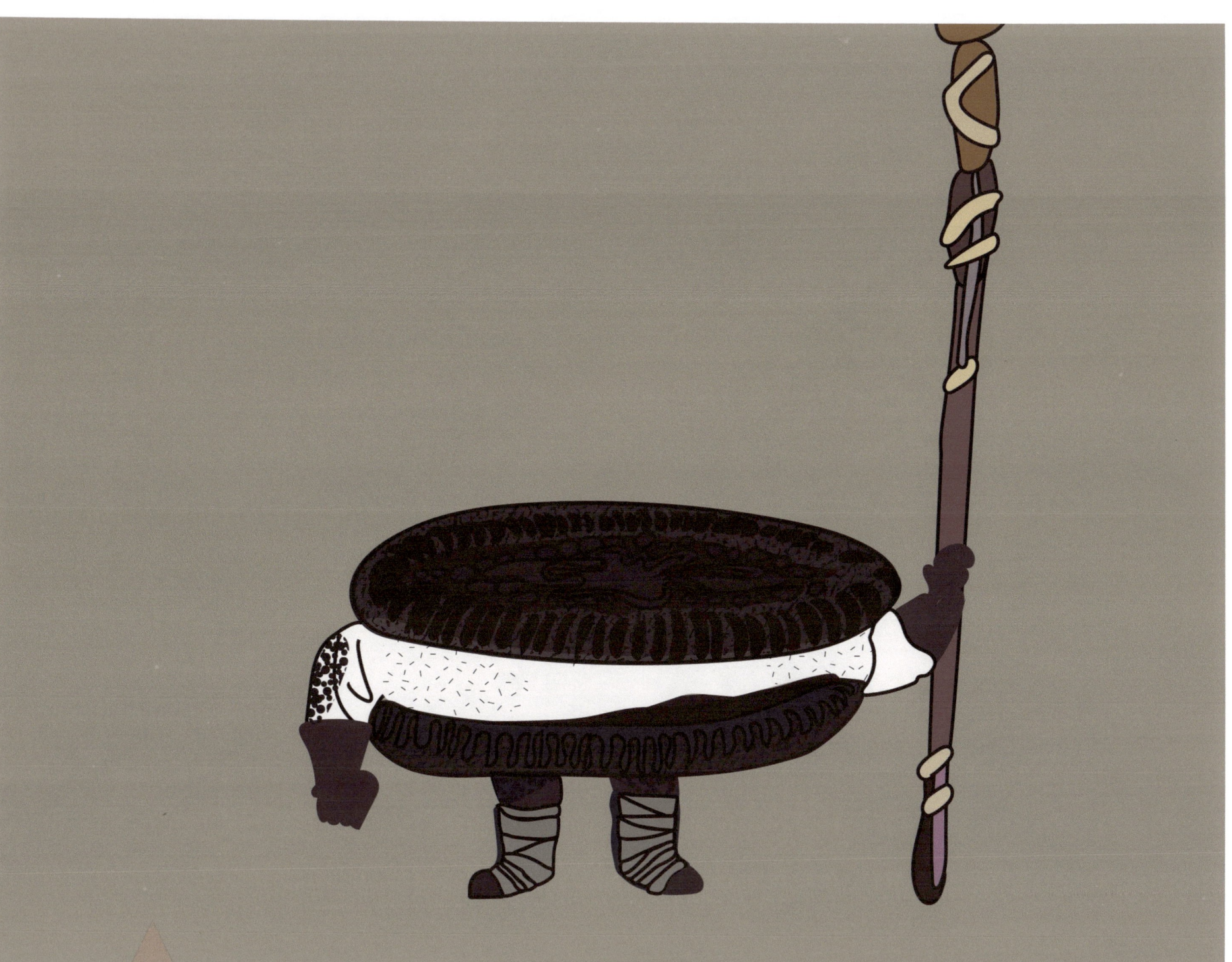

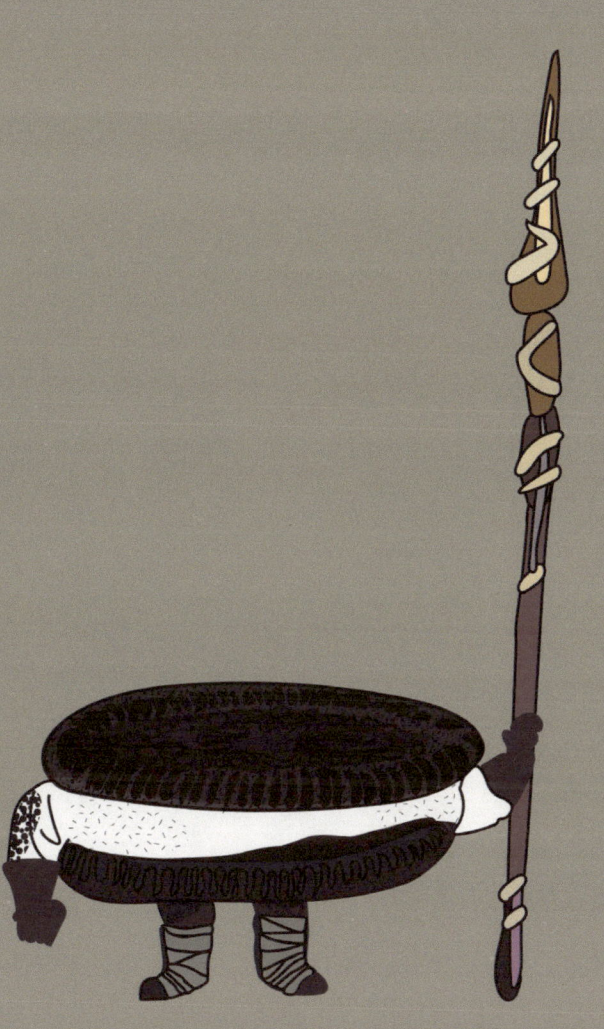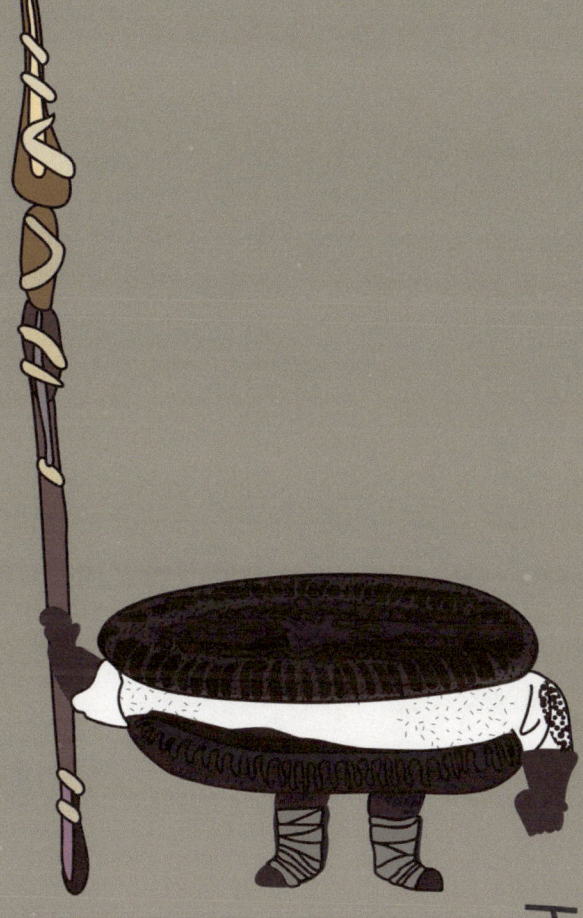

Justin
V.

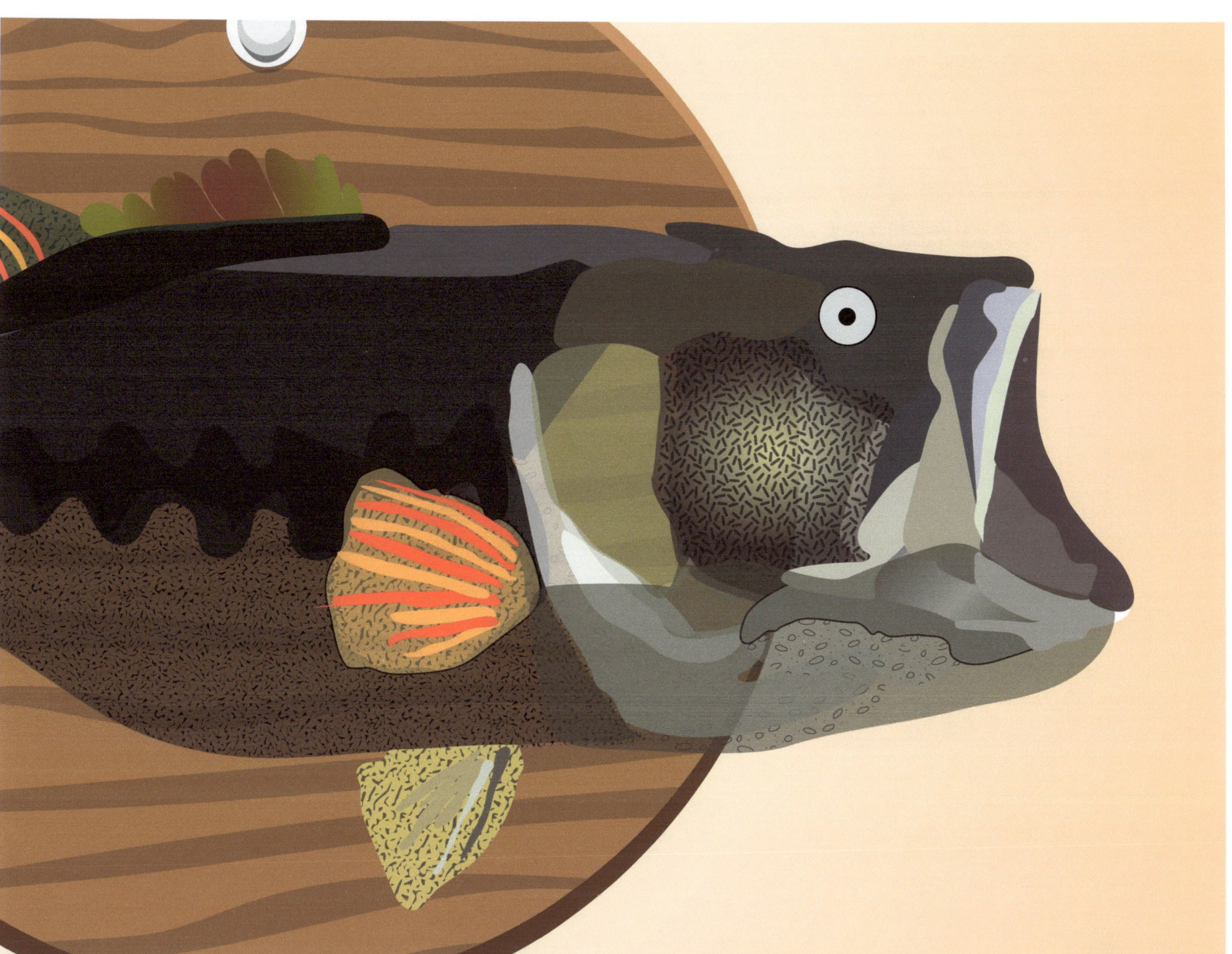

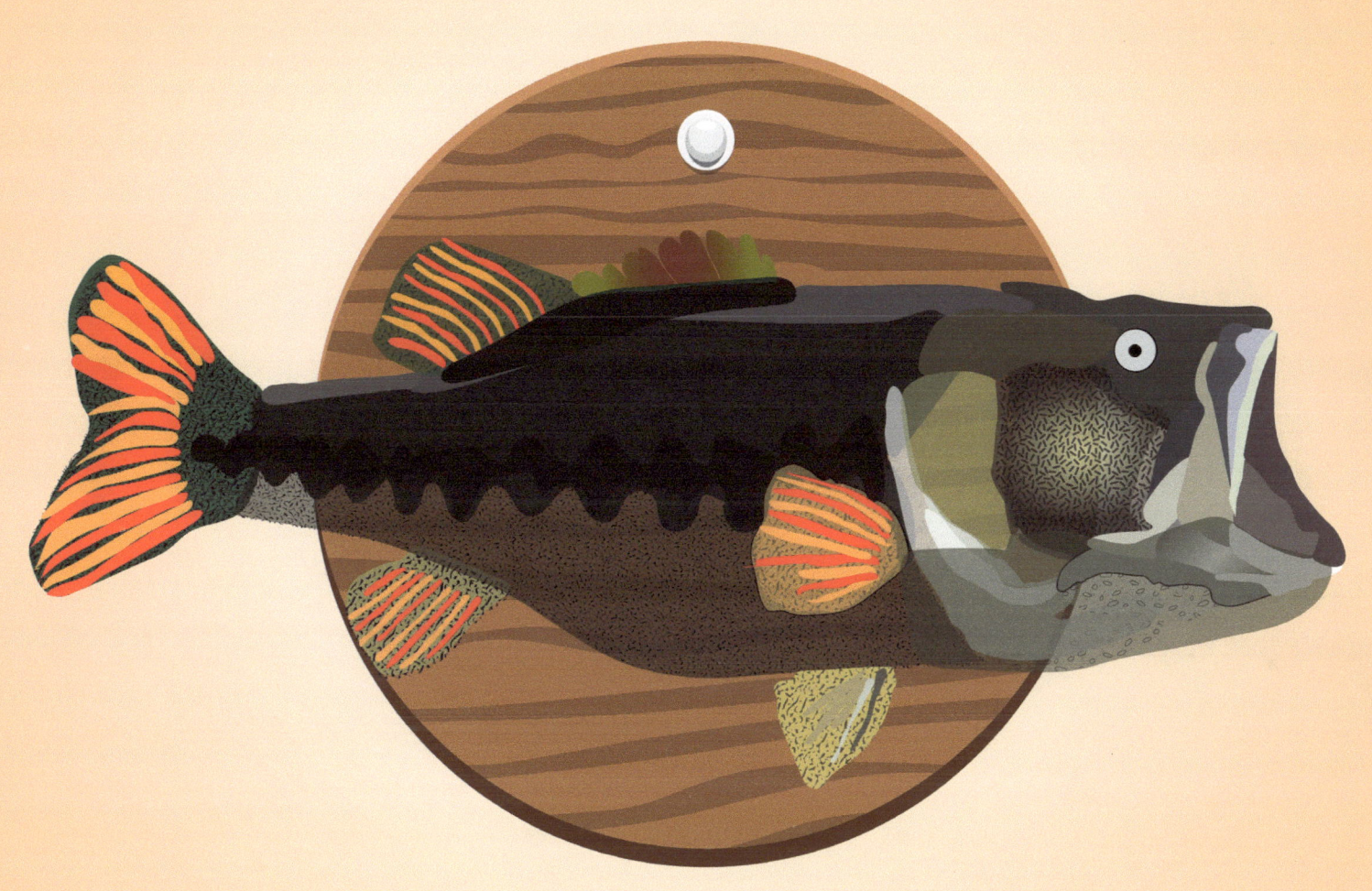

Justin V.

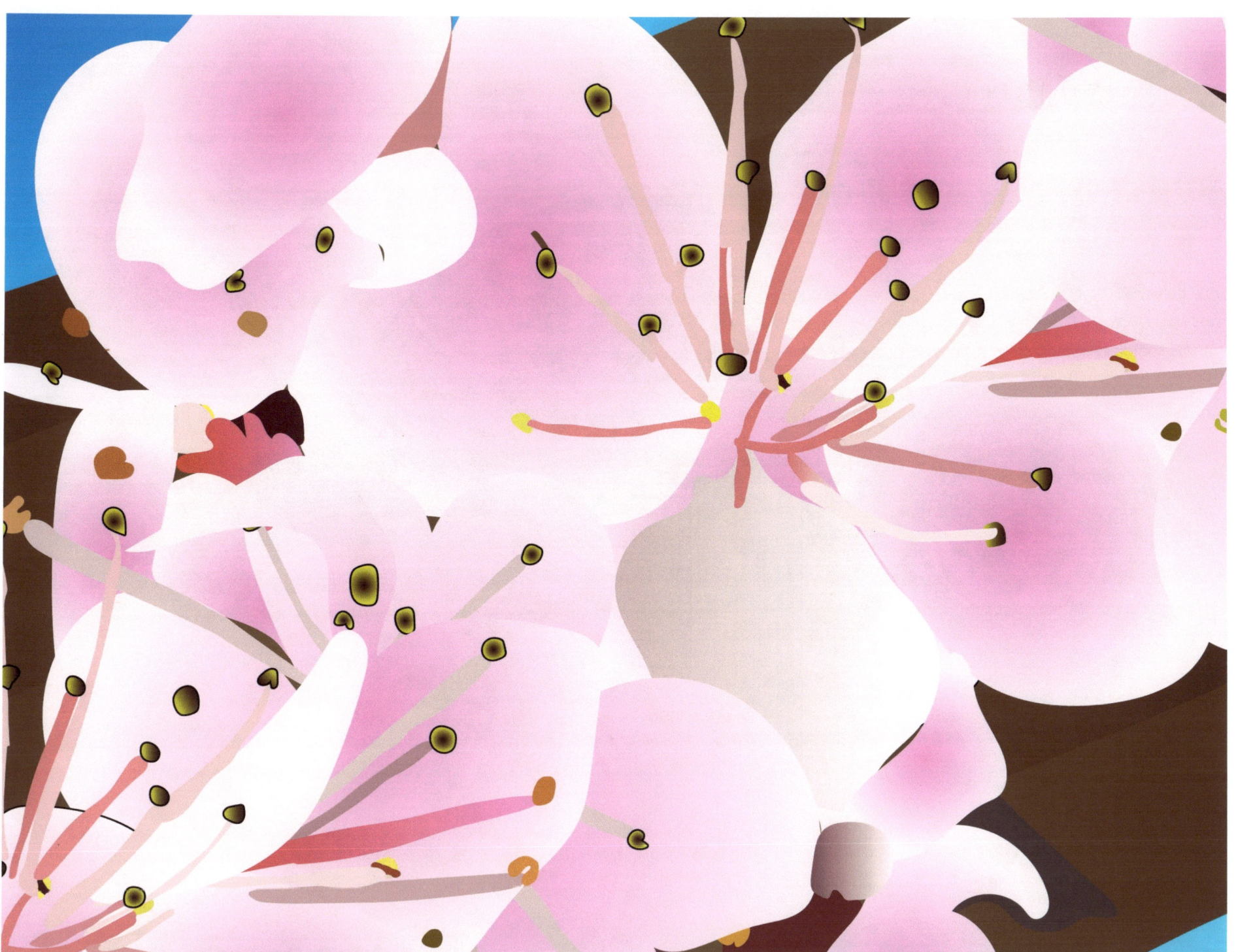

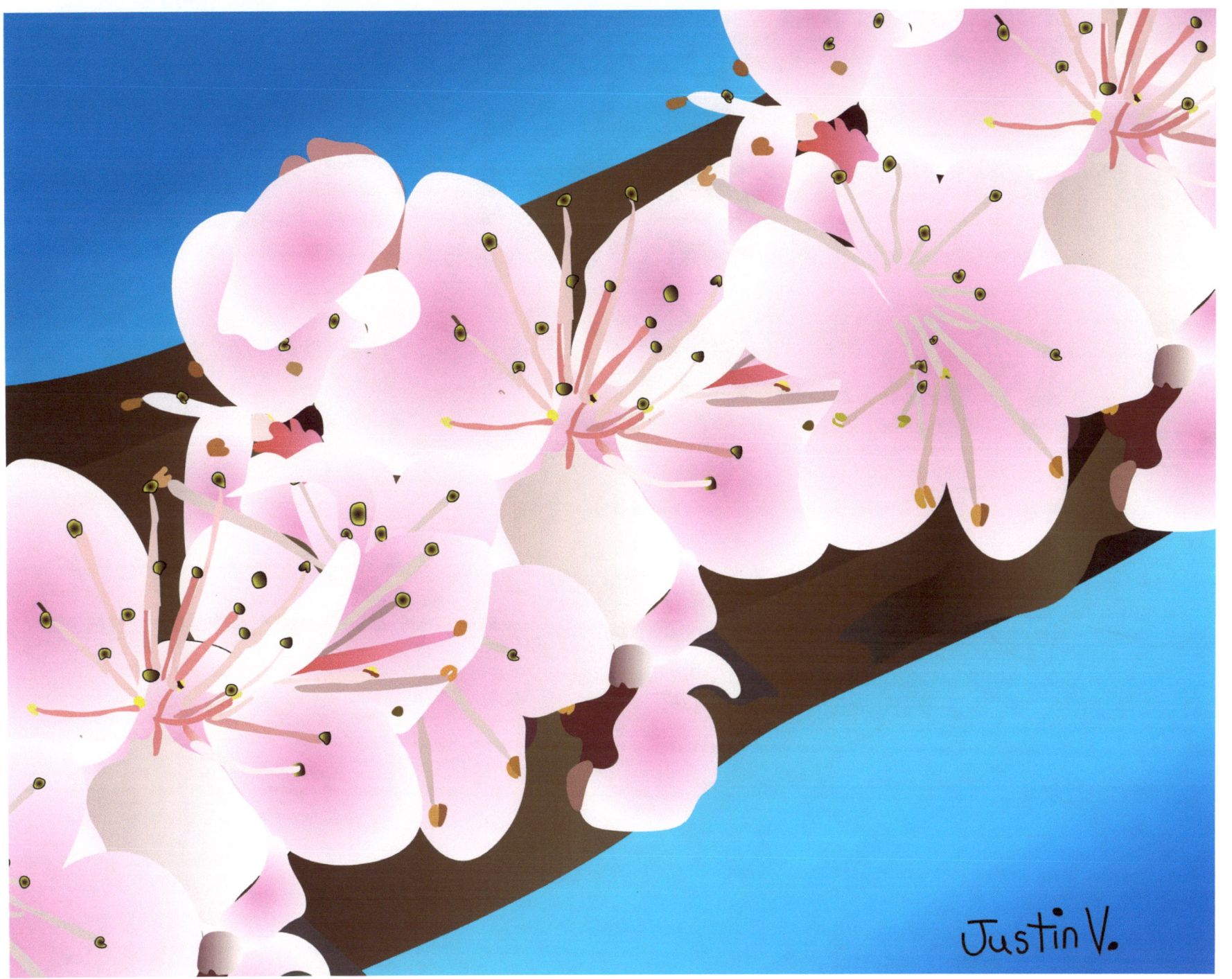

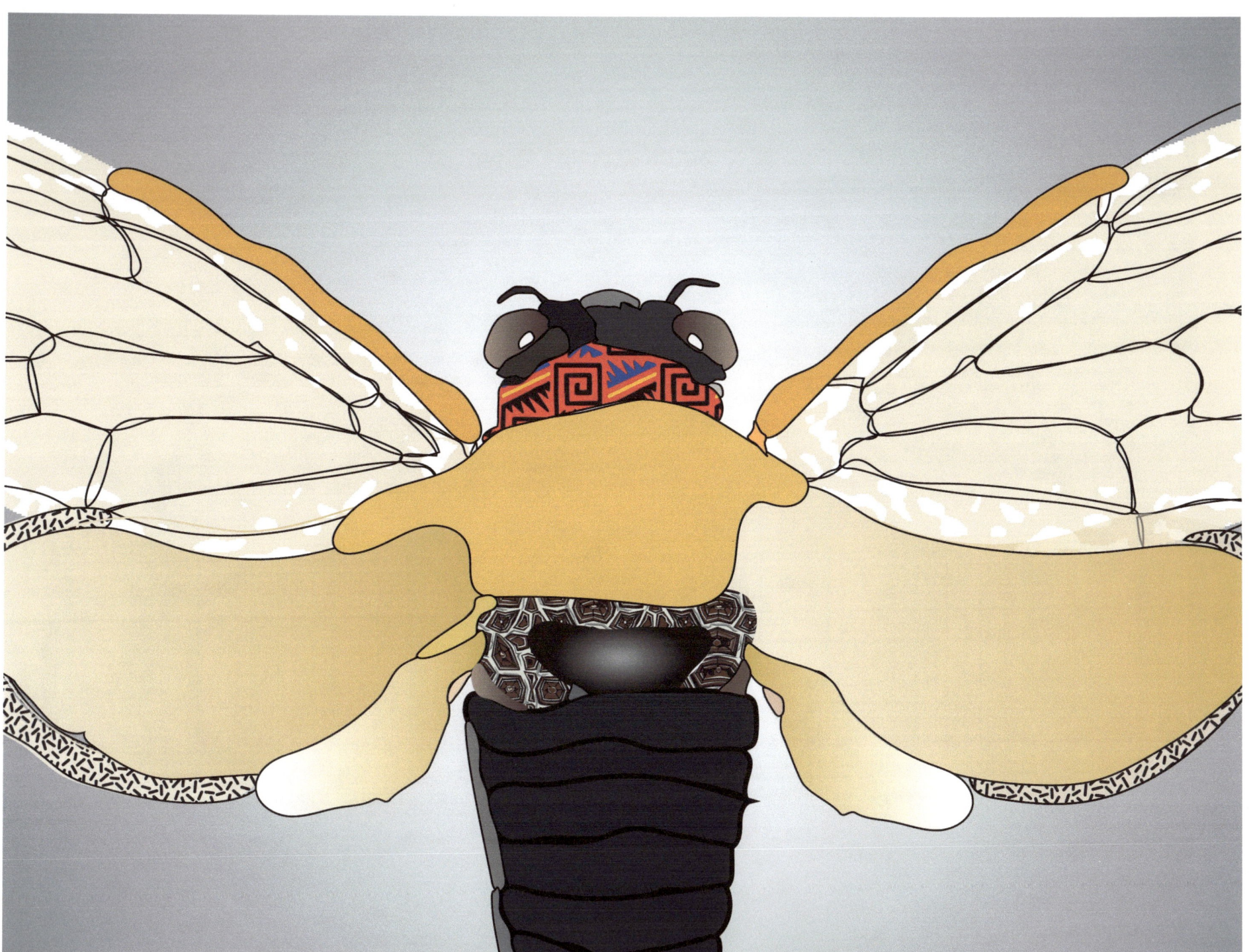

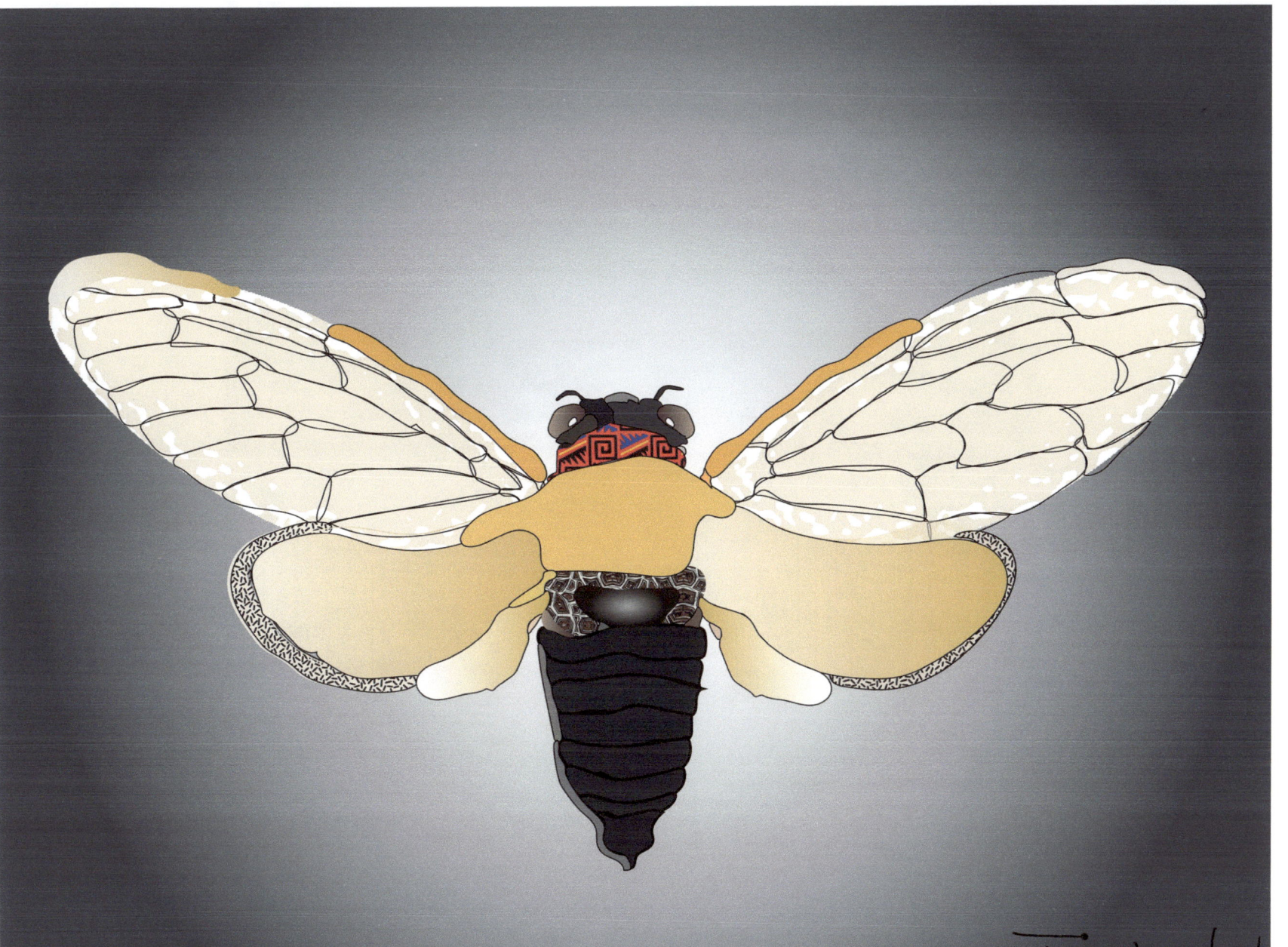

JustinU.

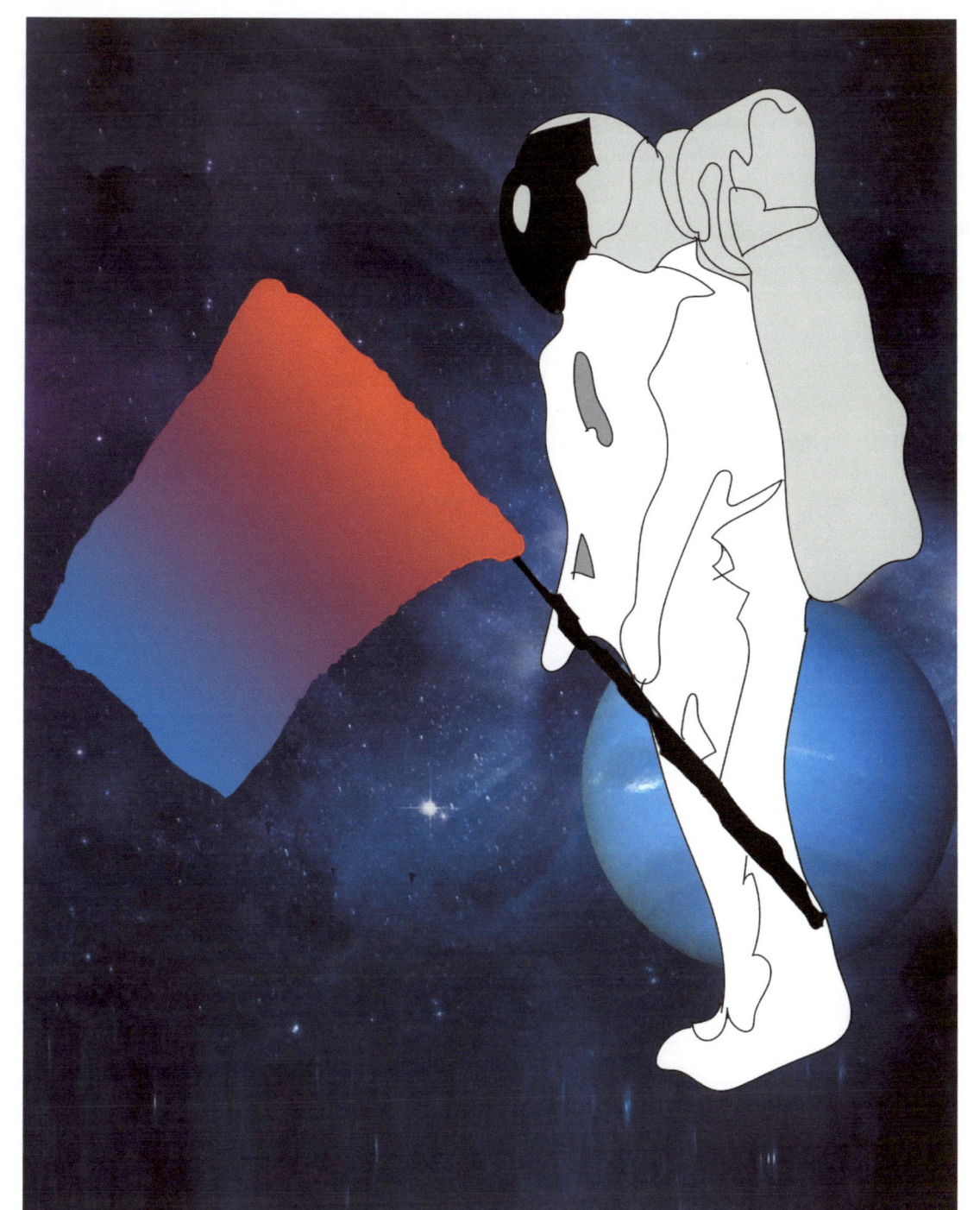

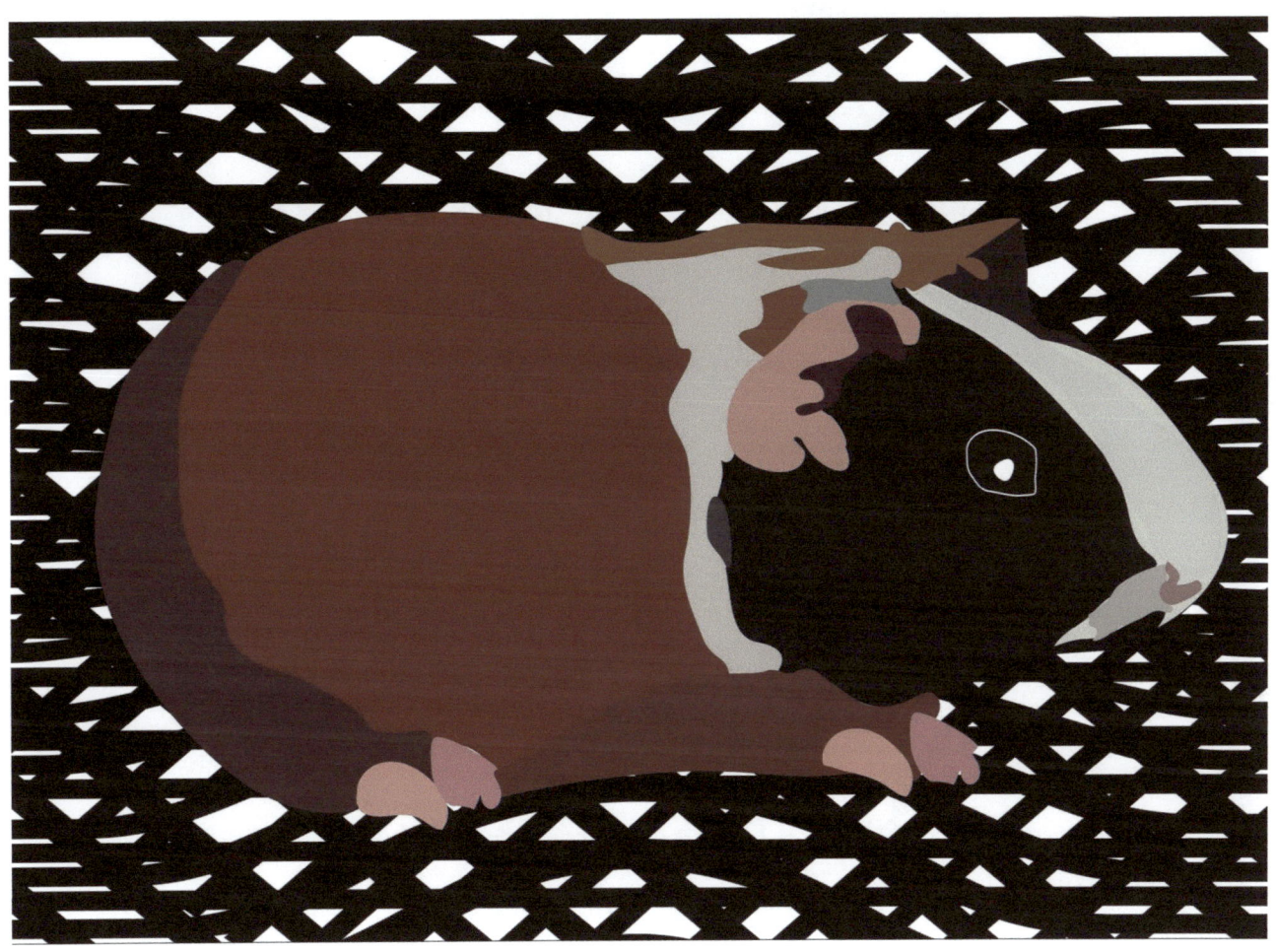

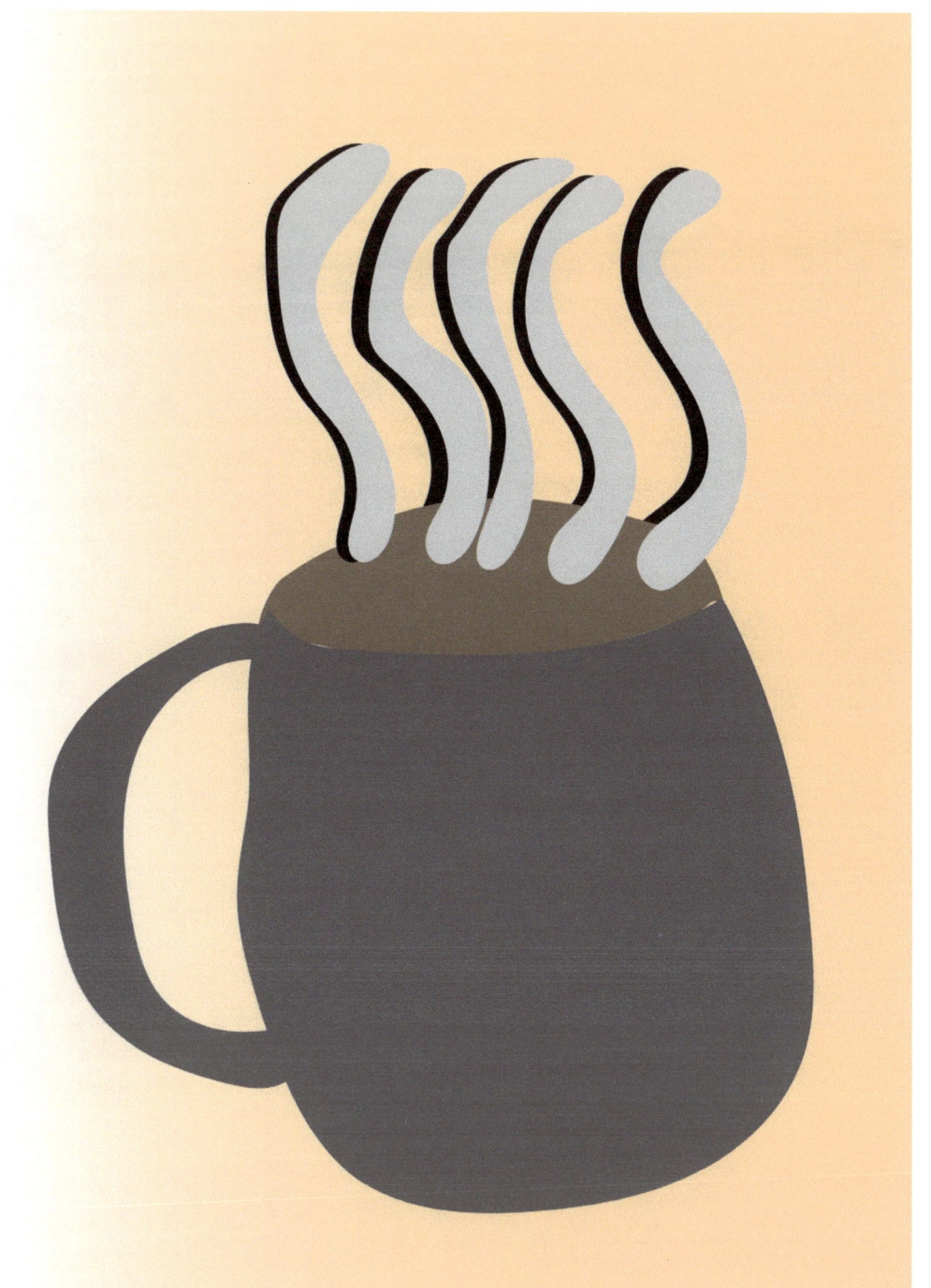

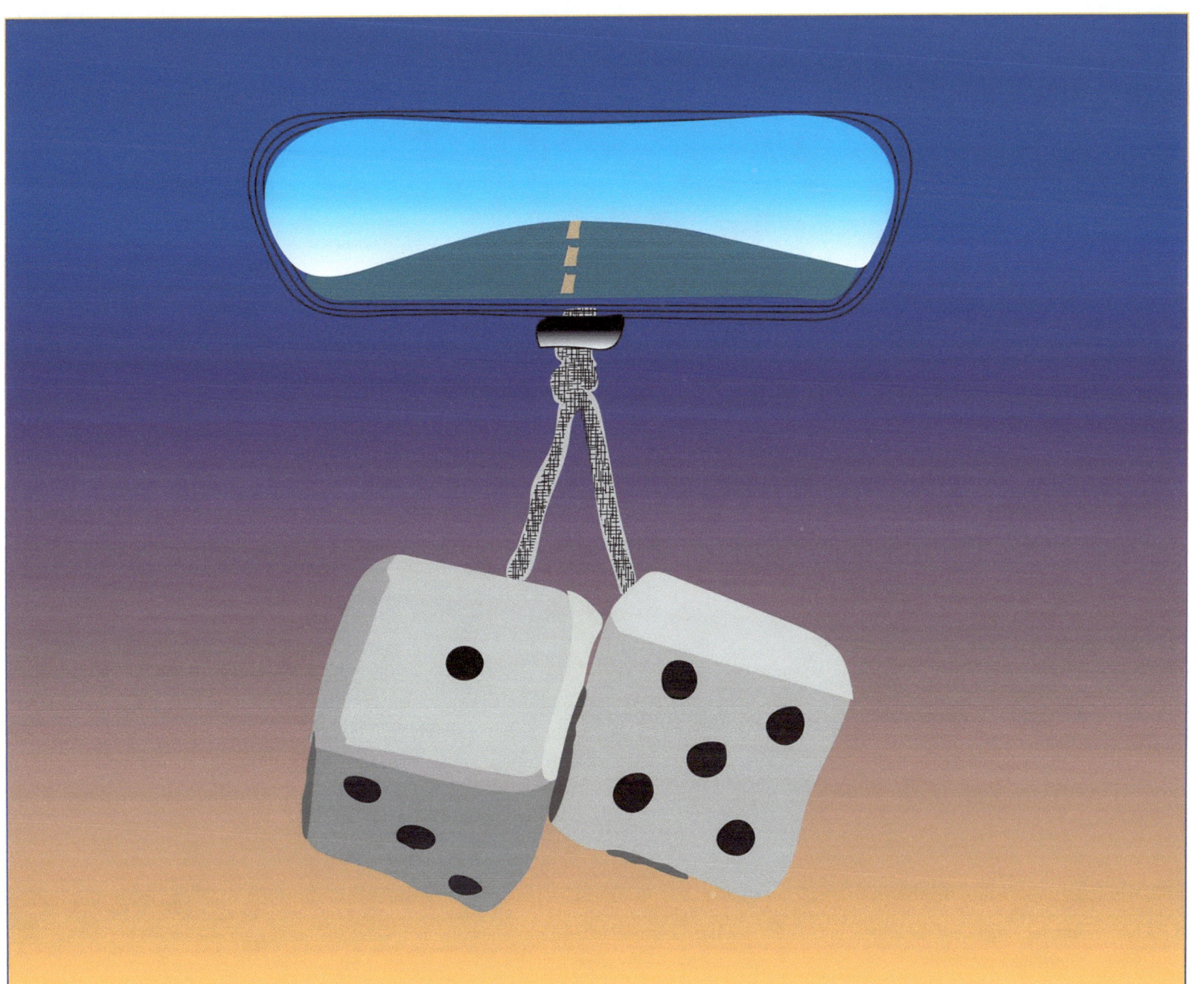

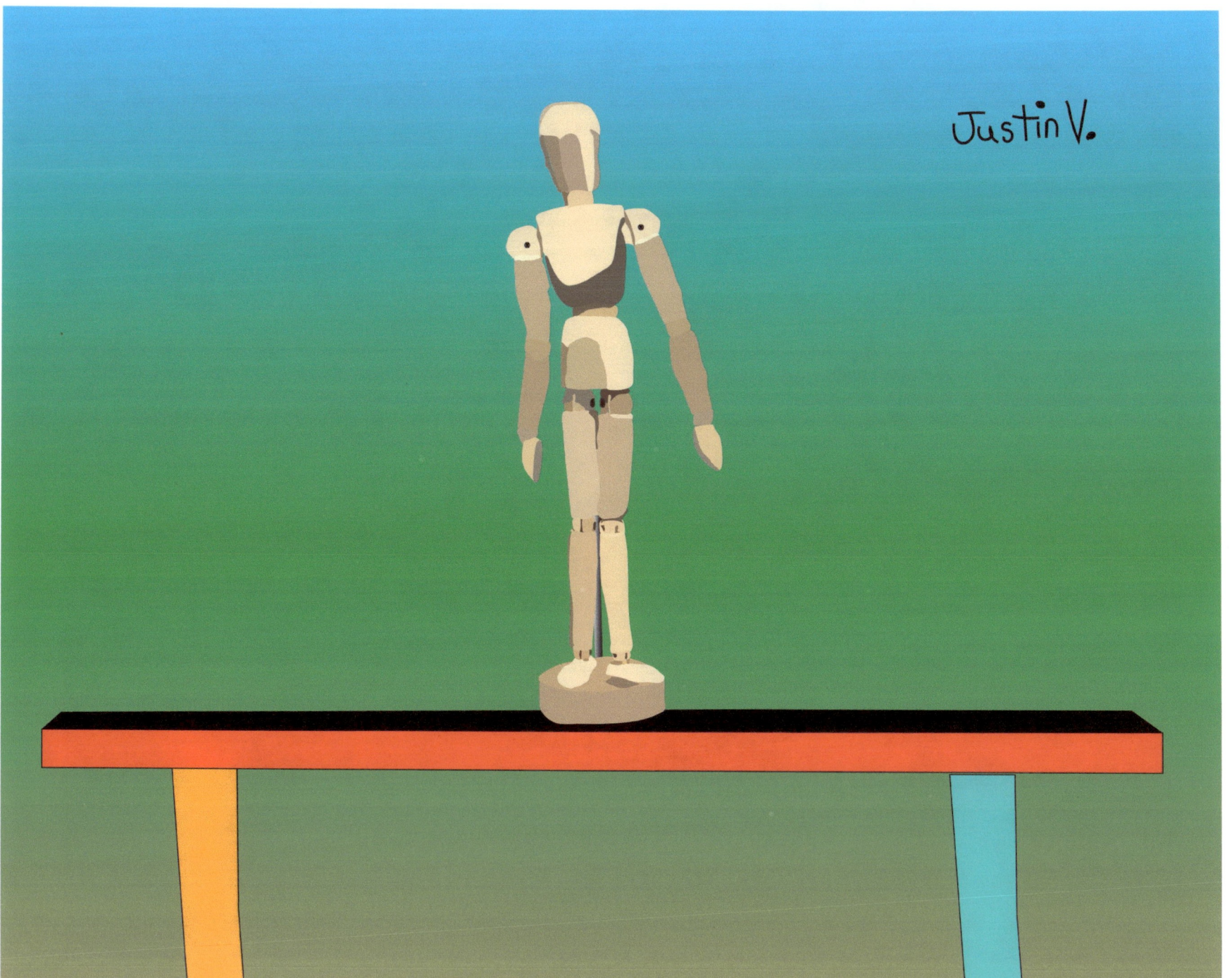

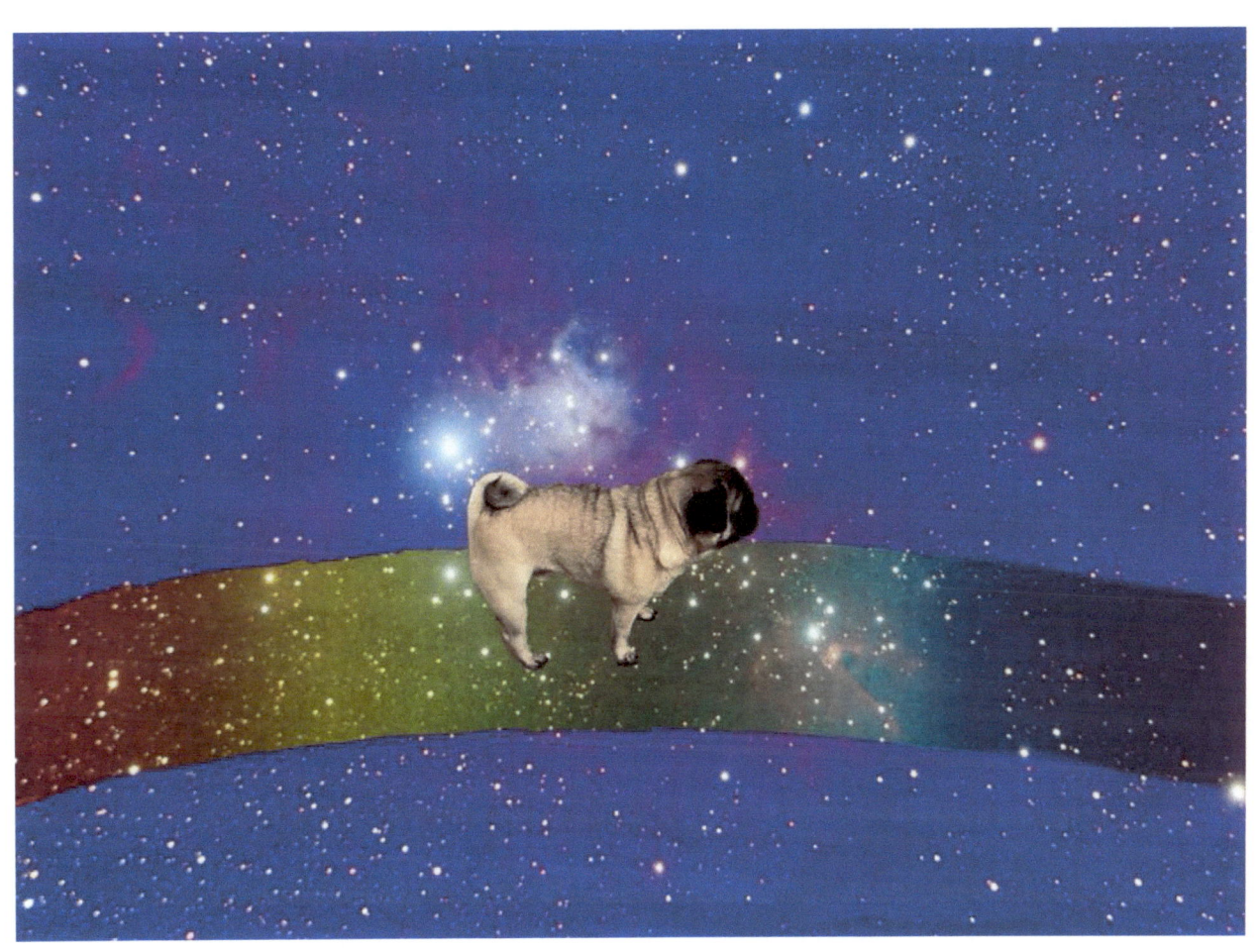

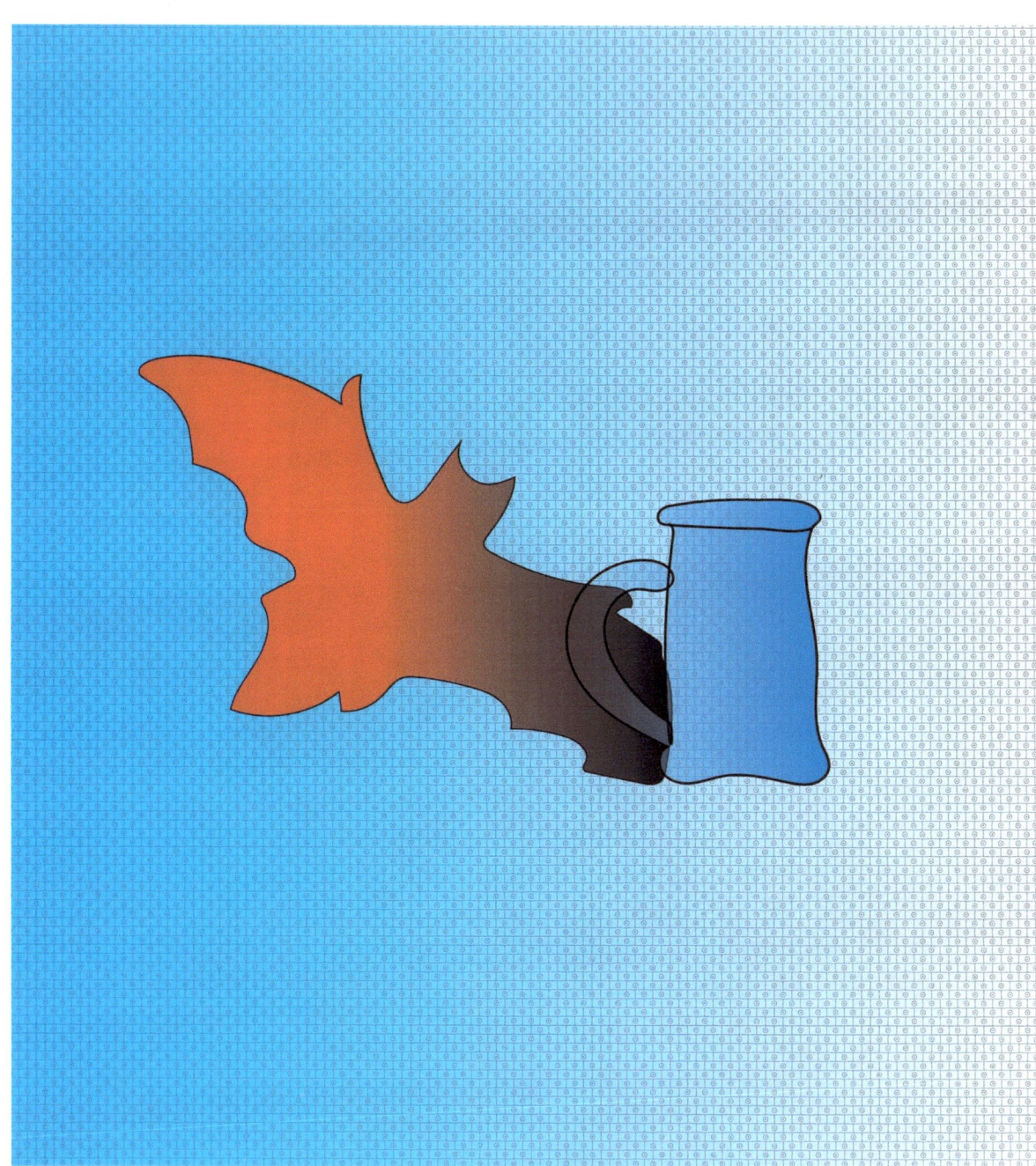

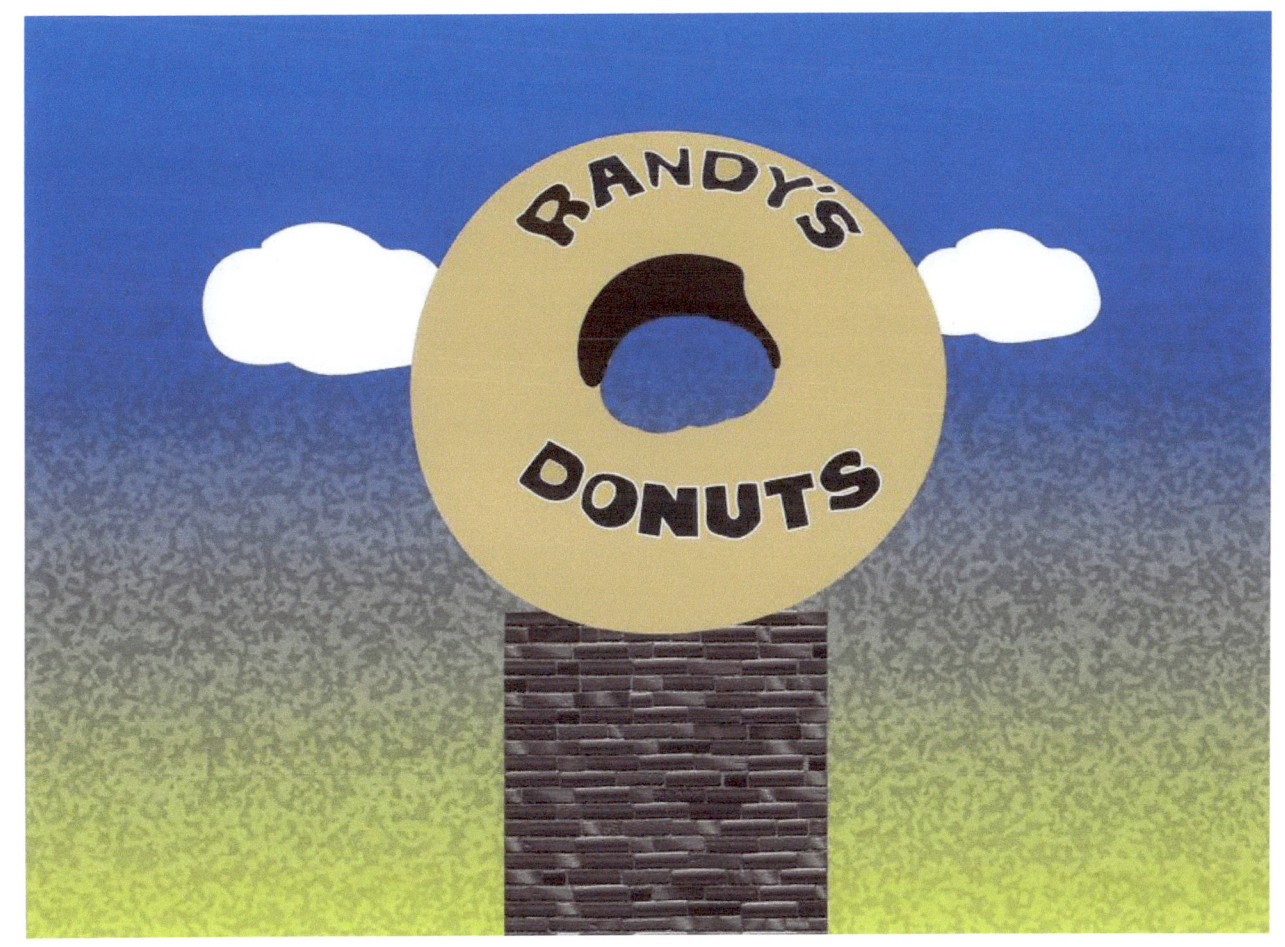

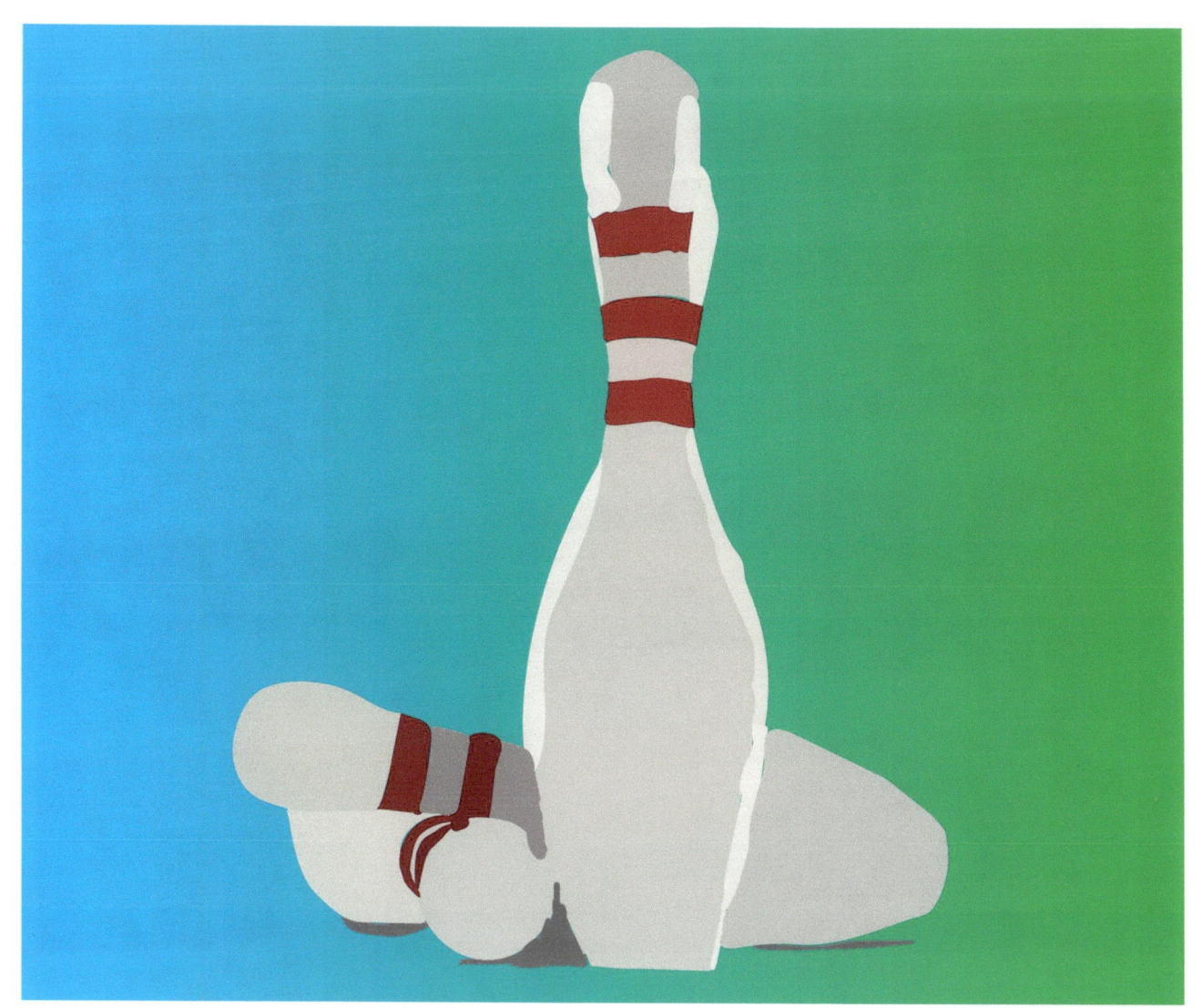

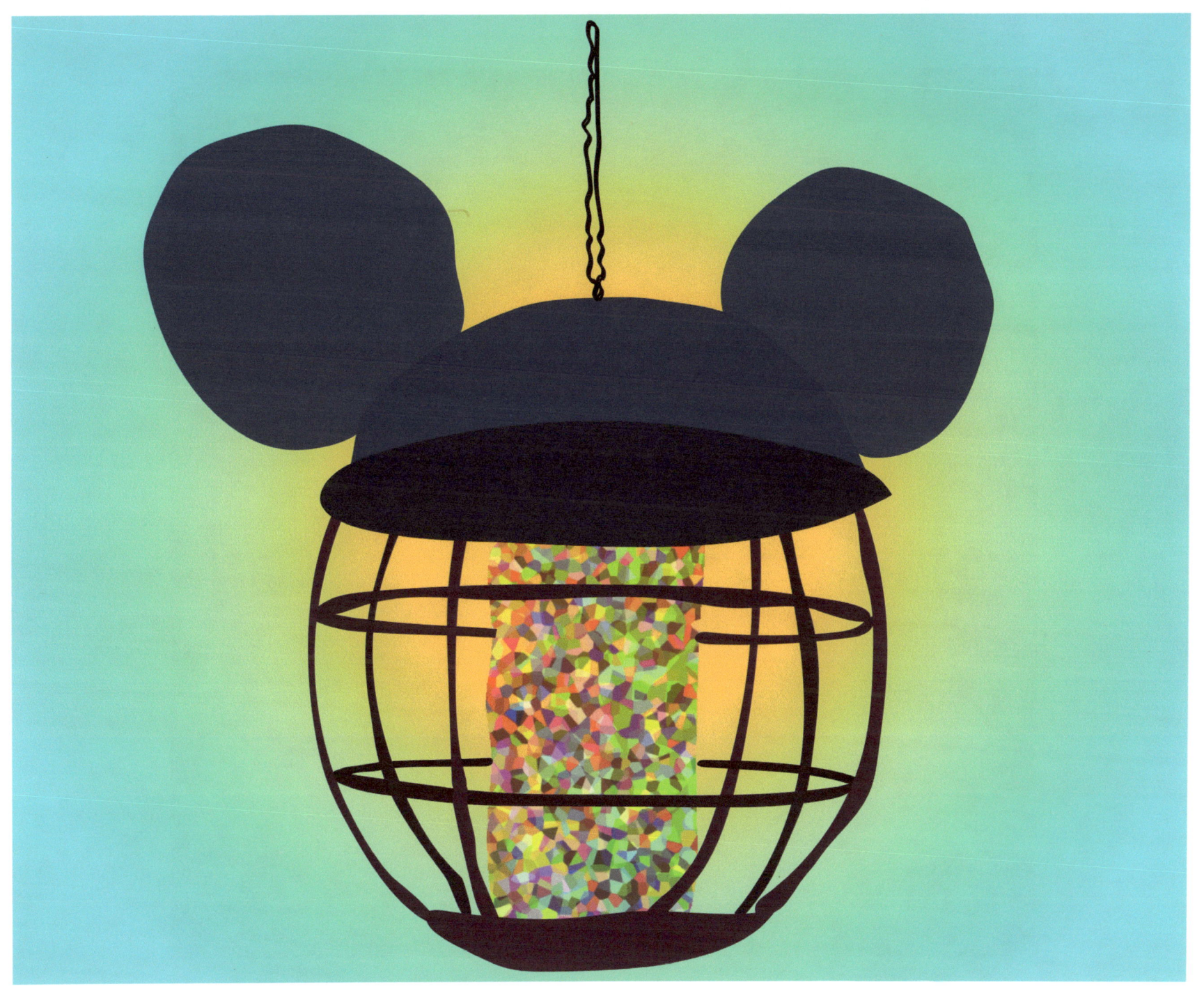

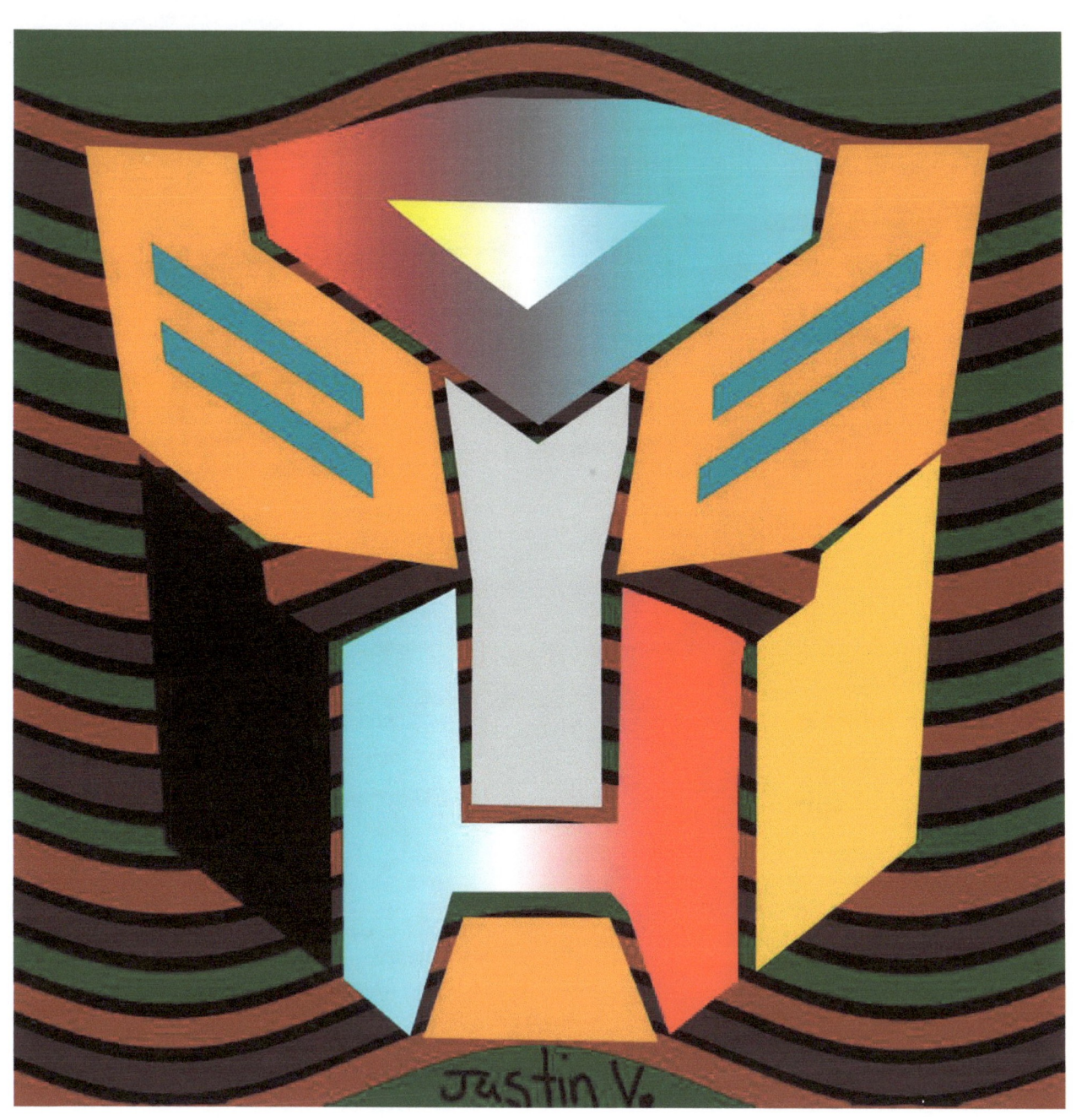

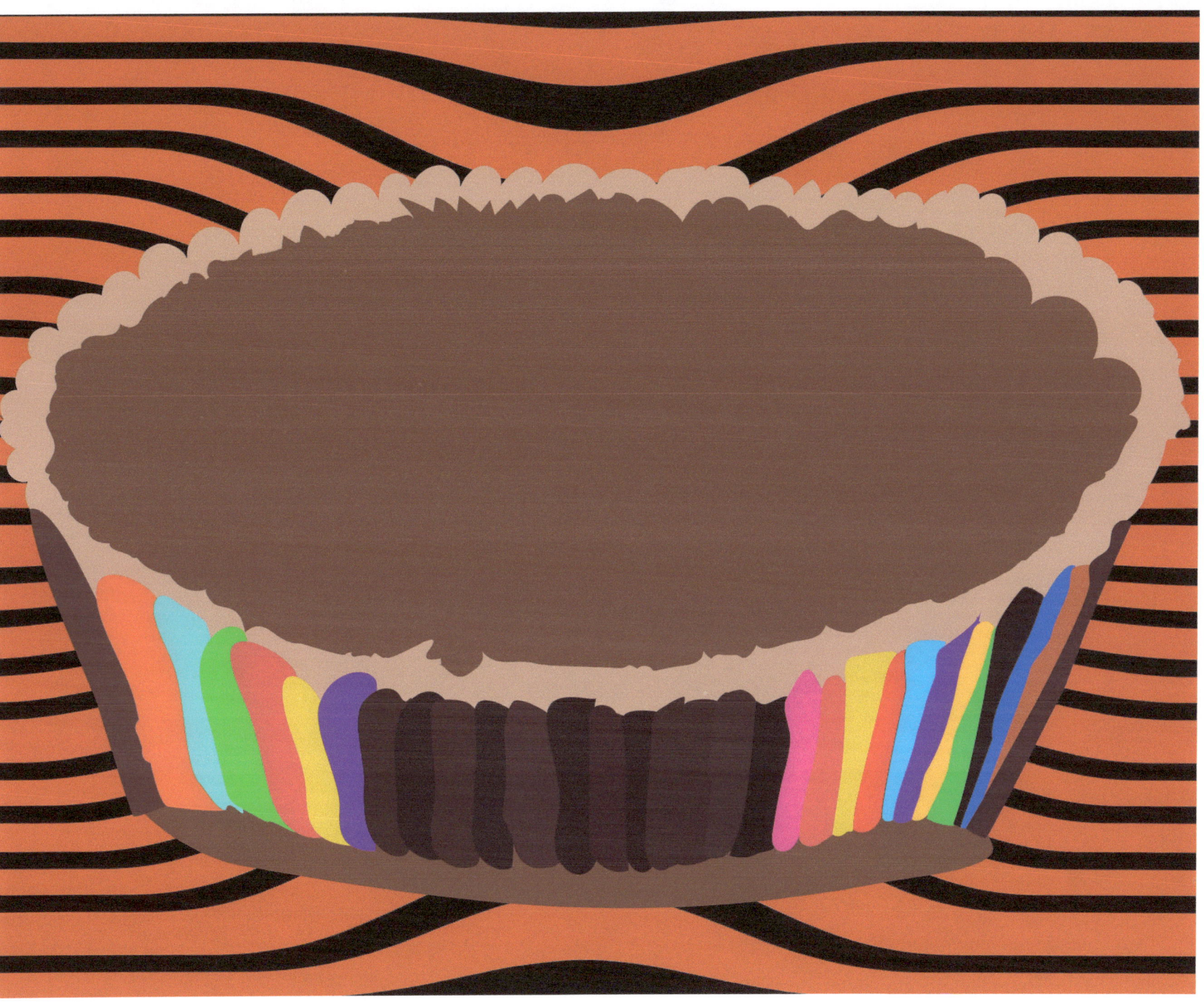

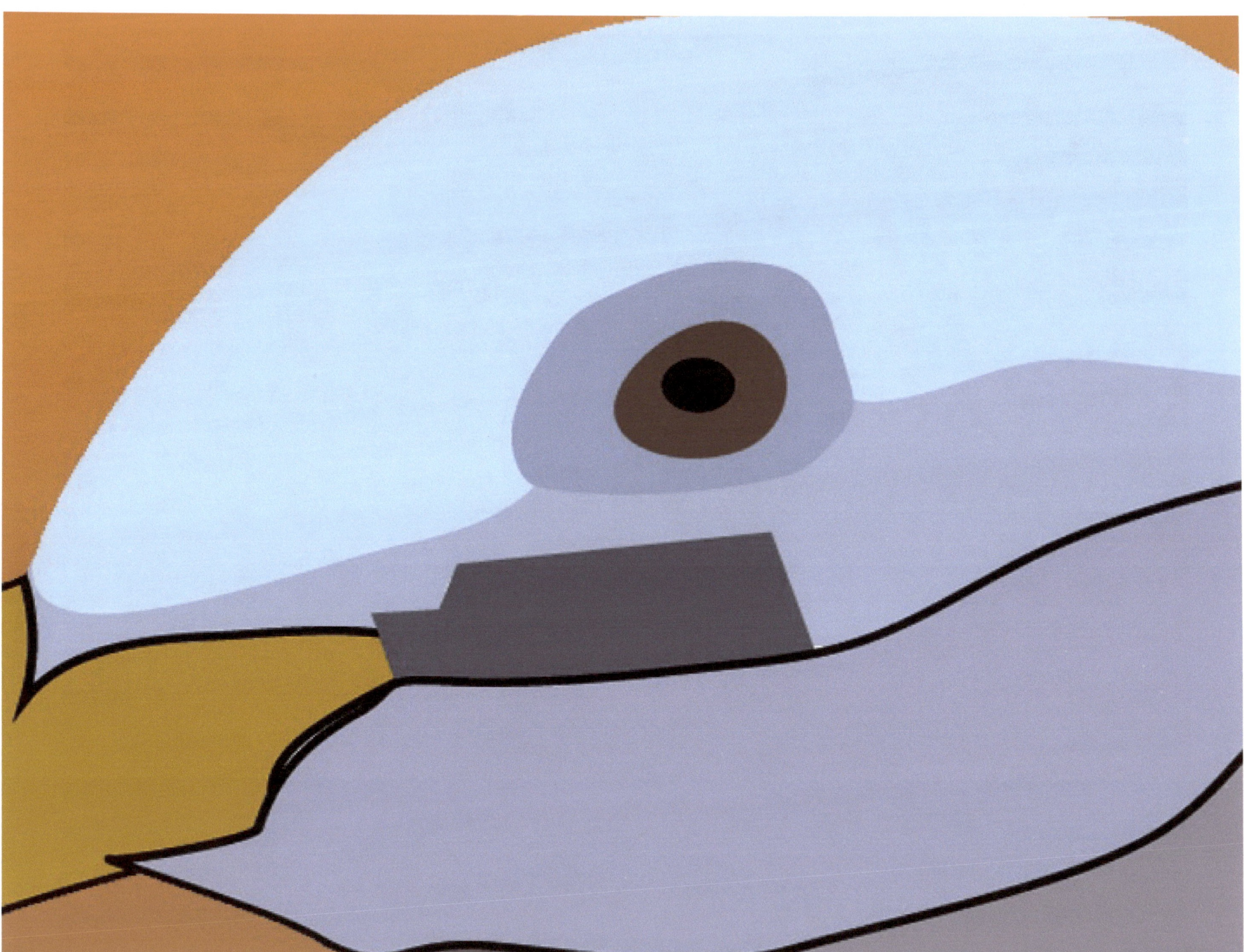

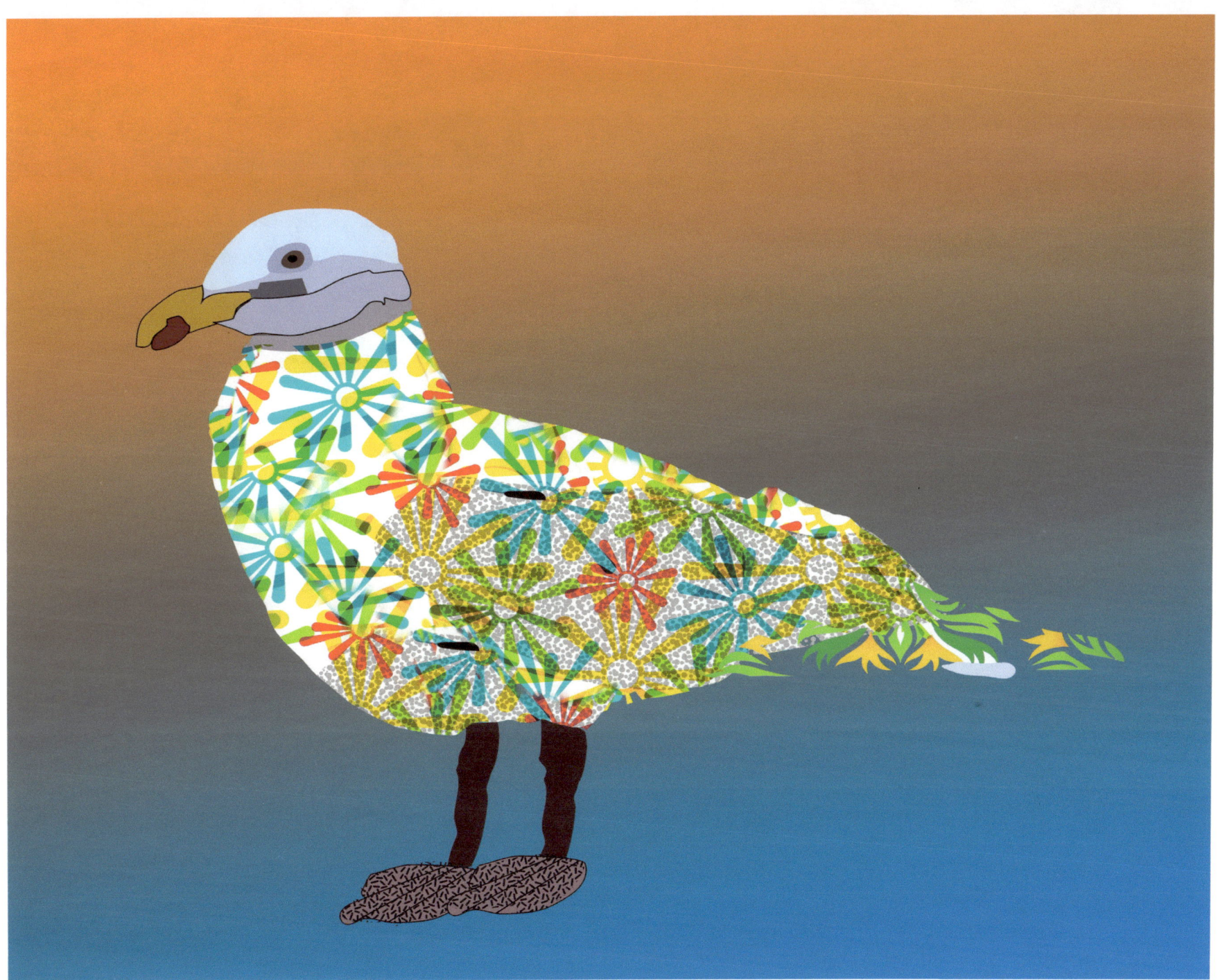

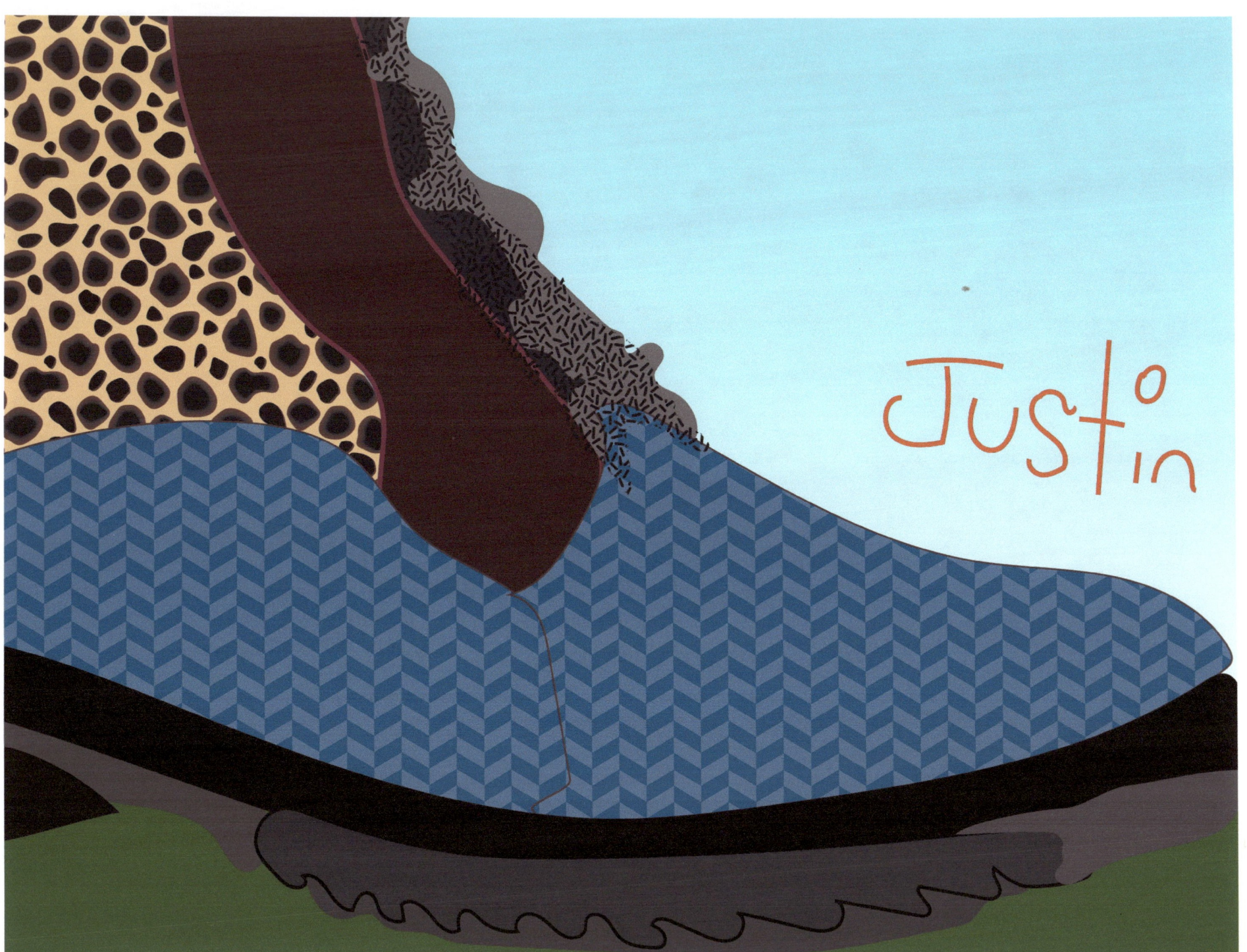

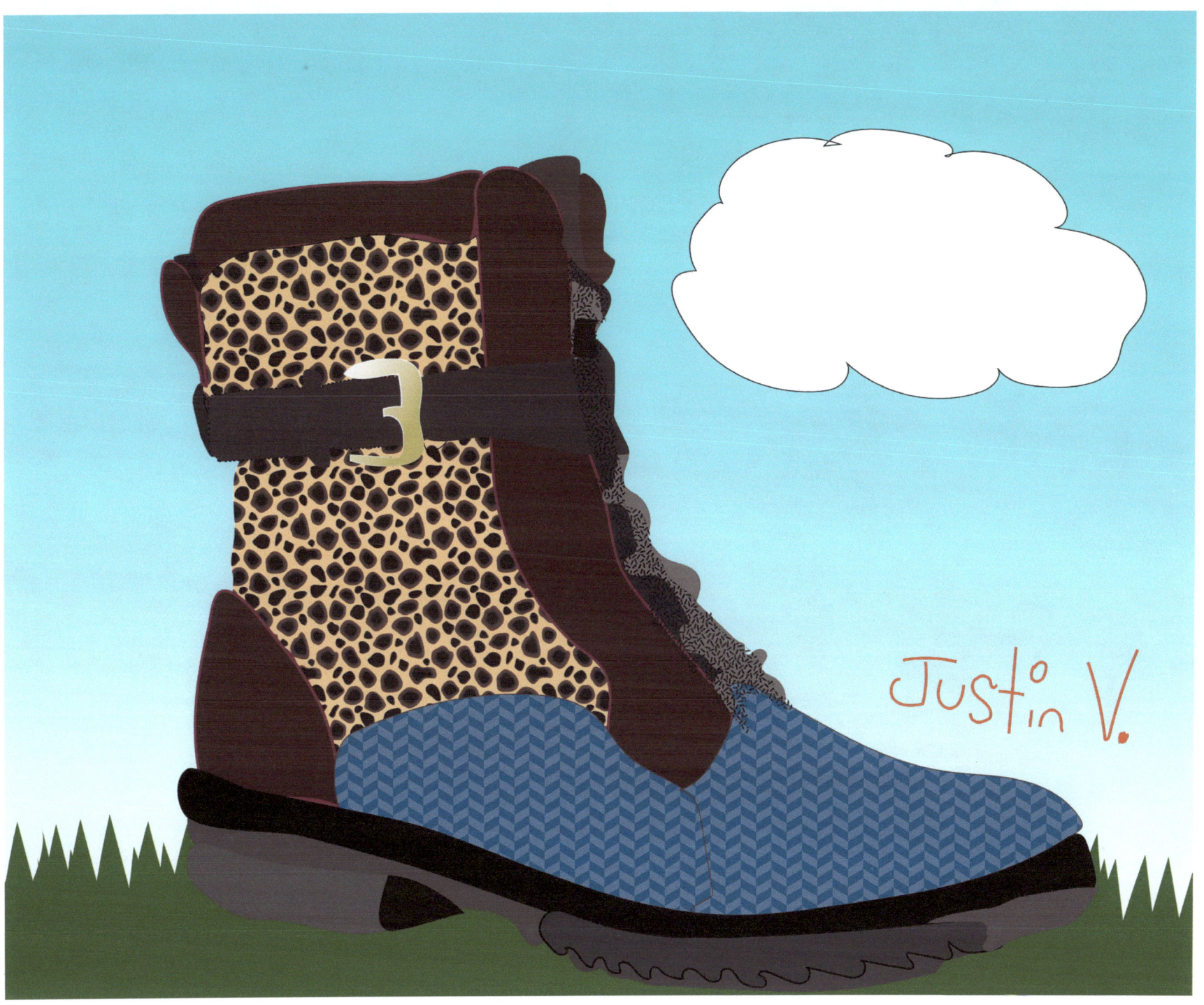

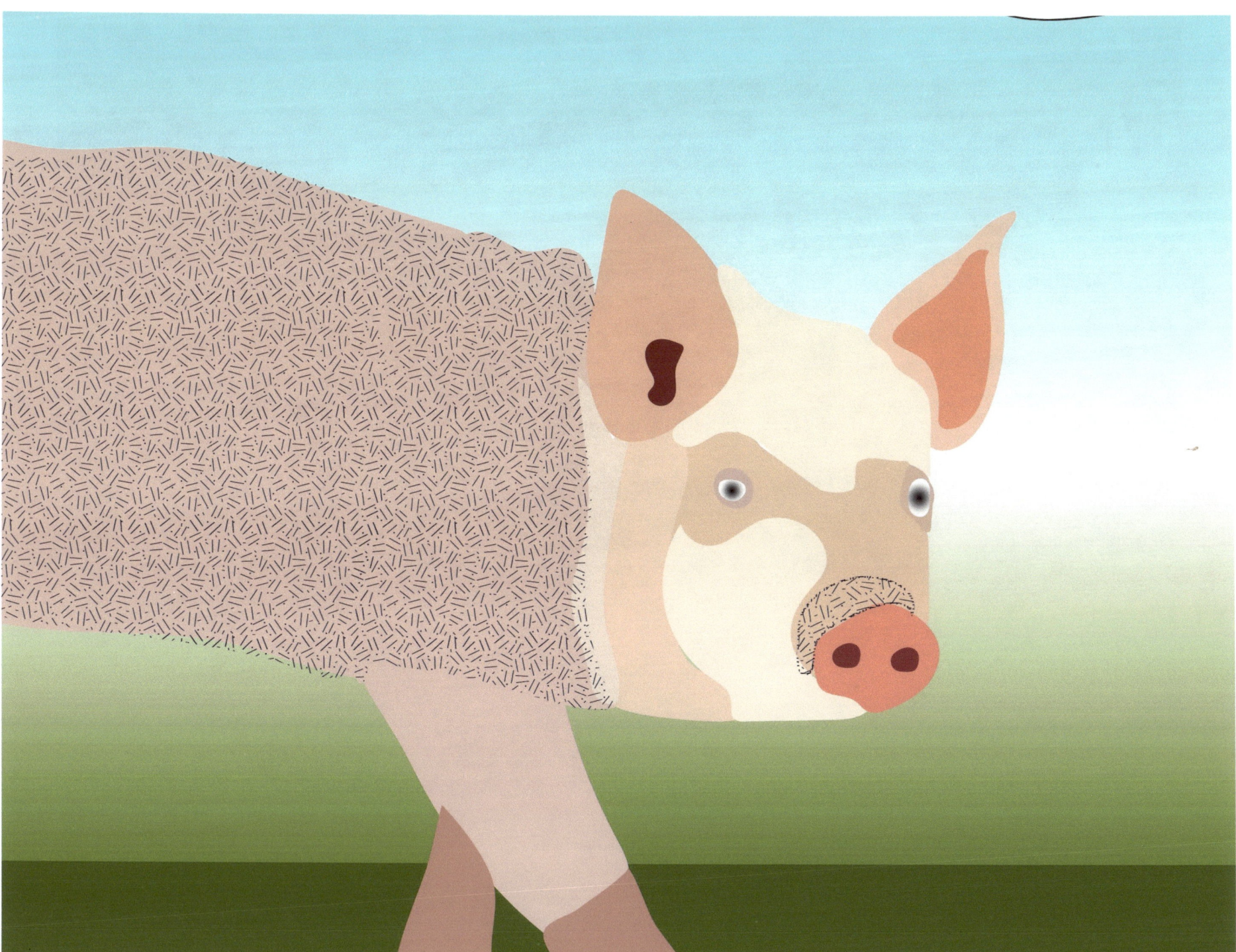

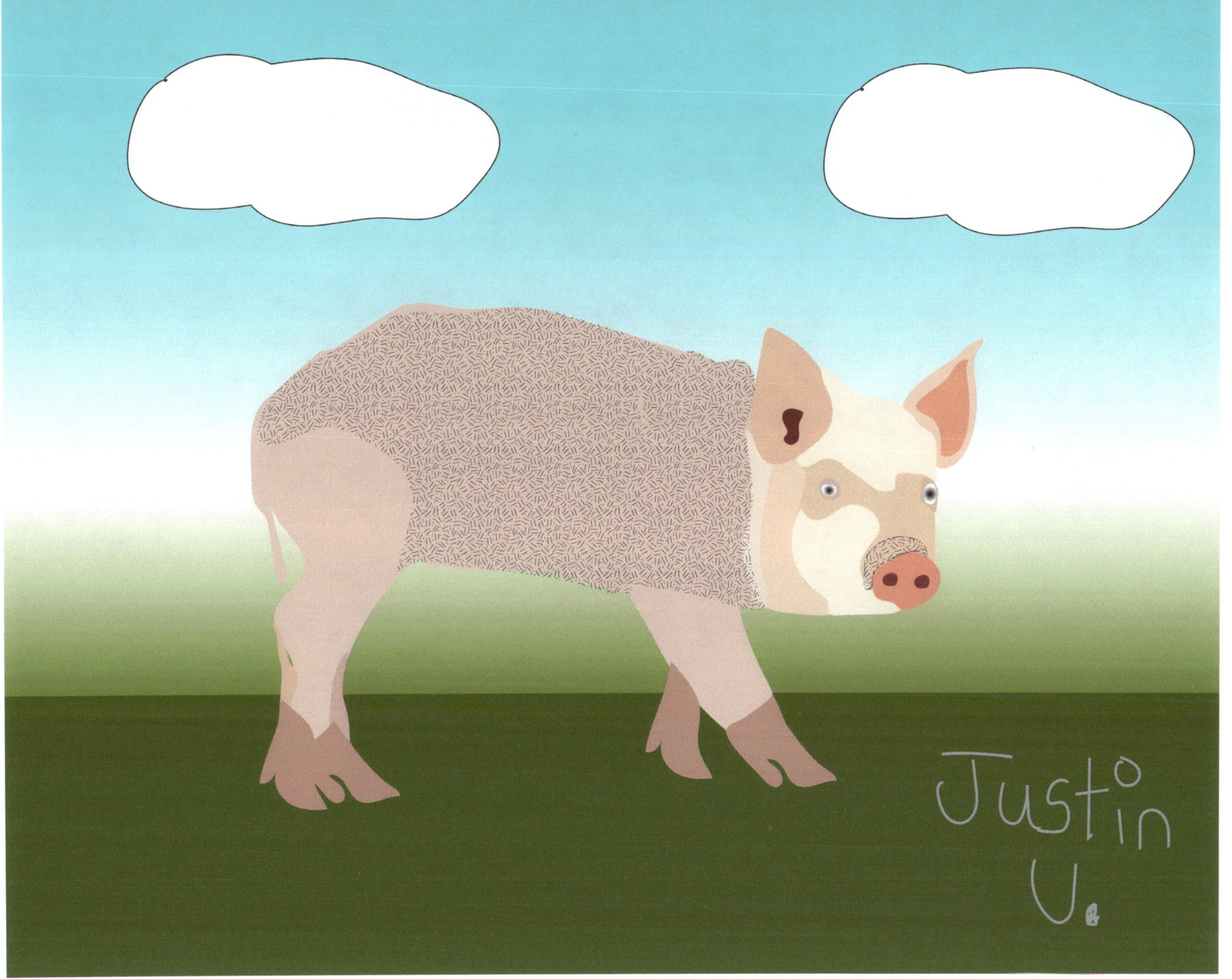

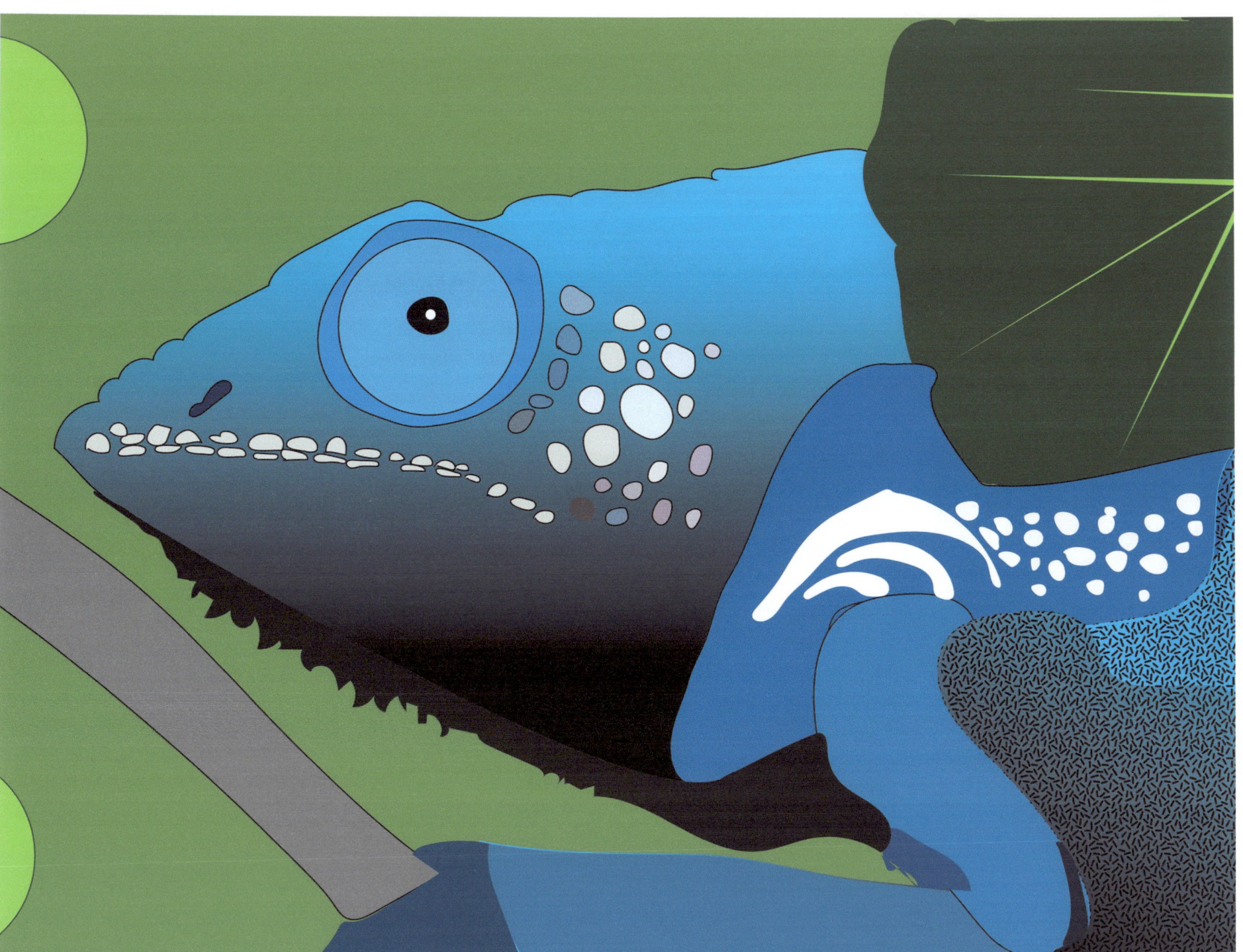

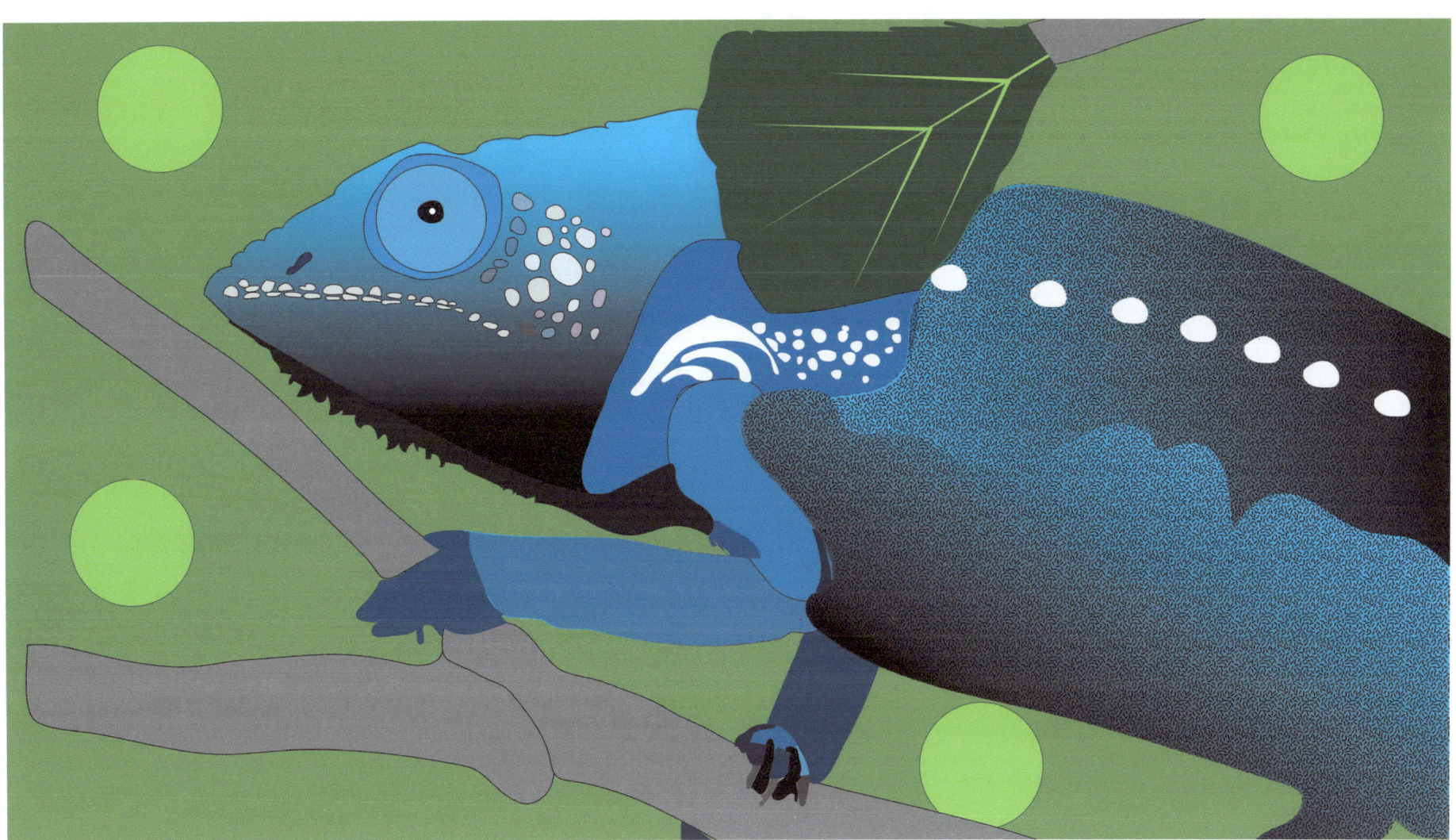

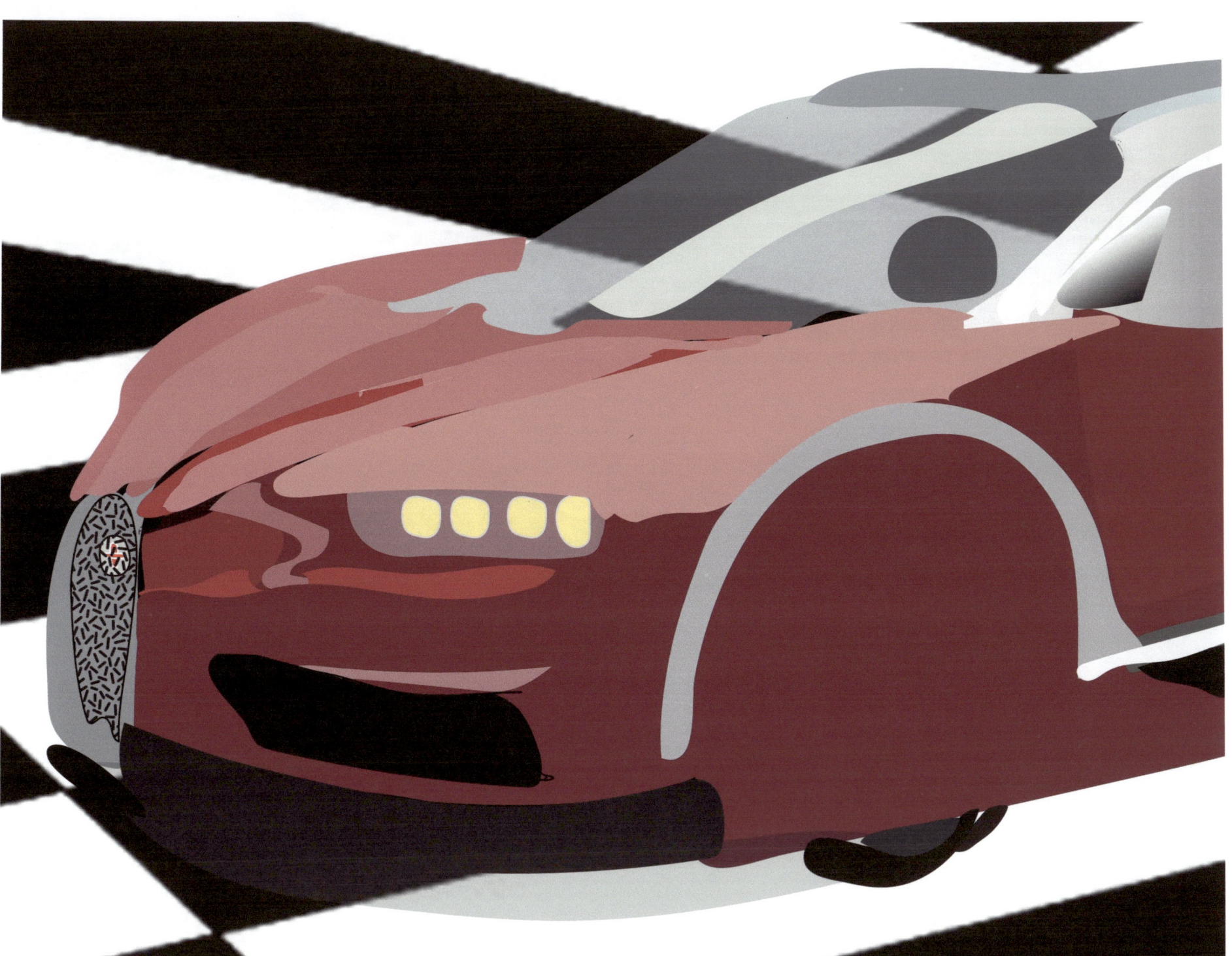

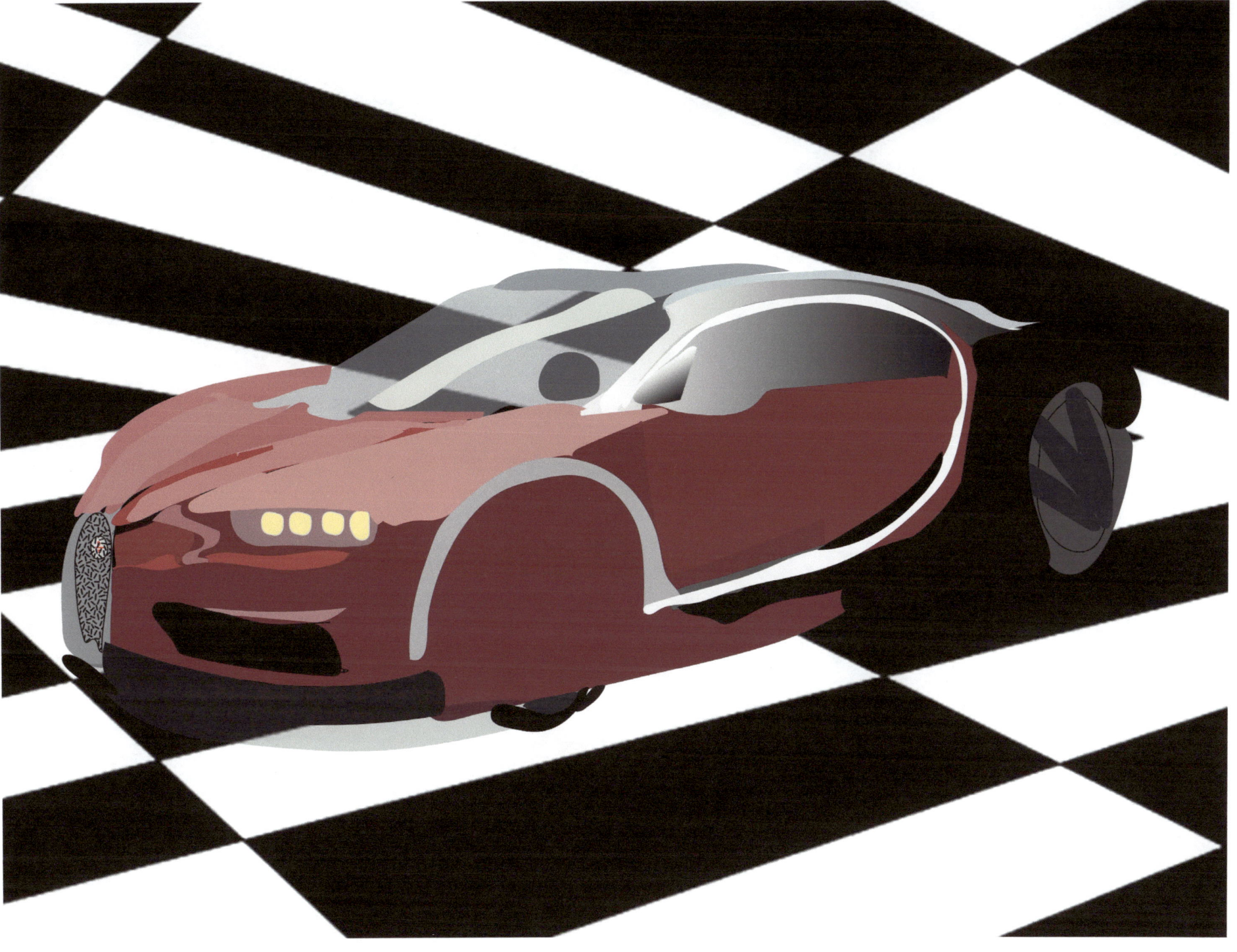

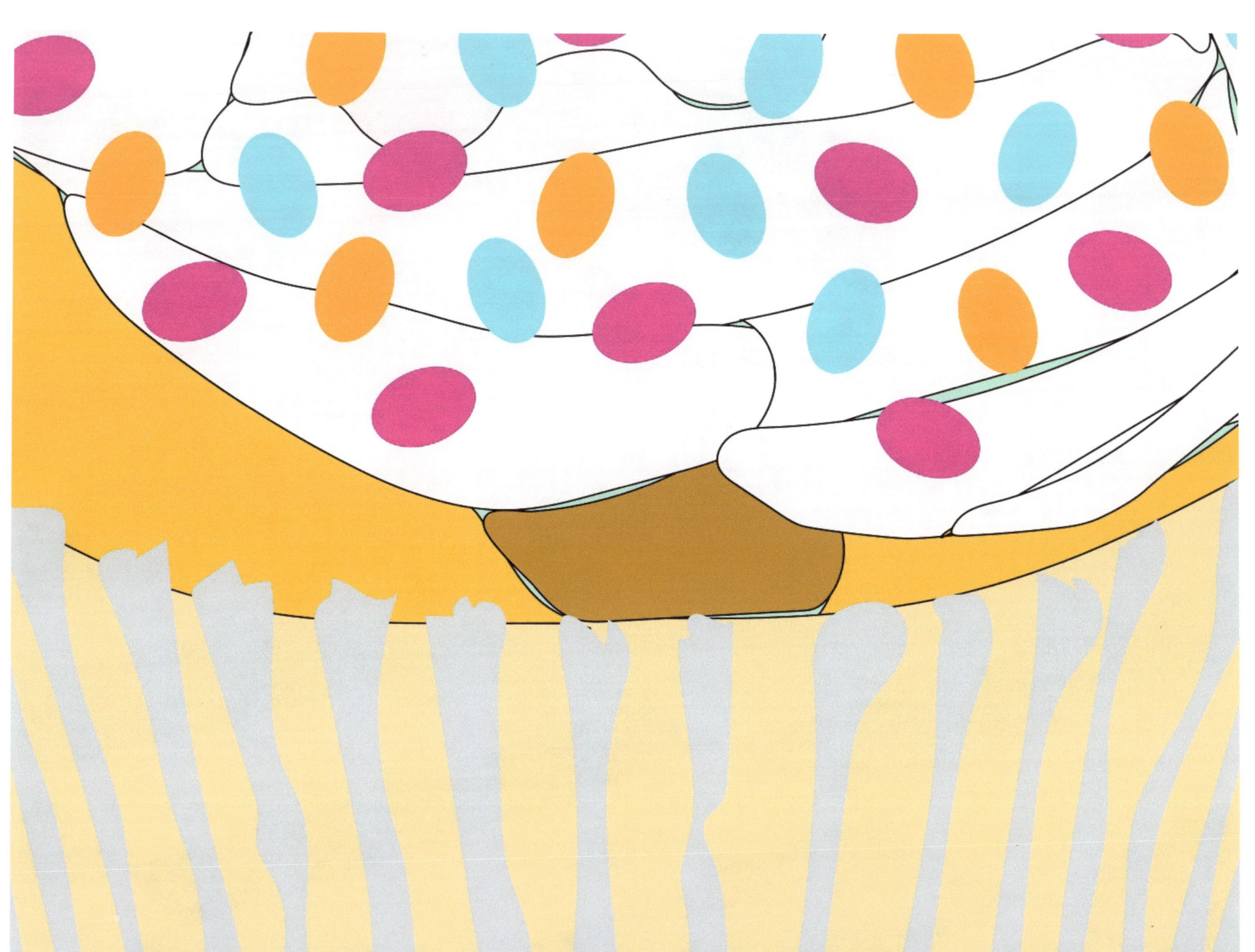

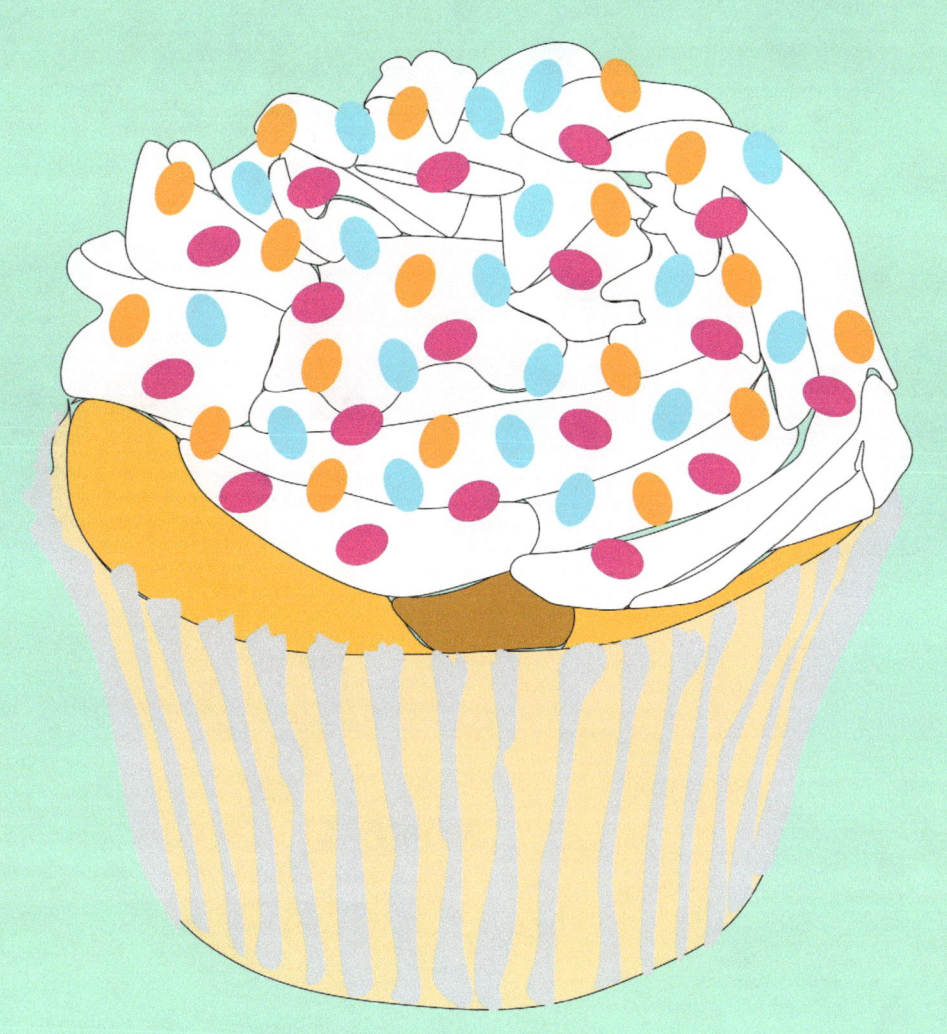

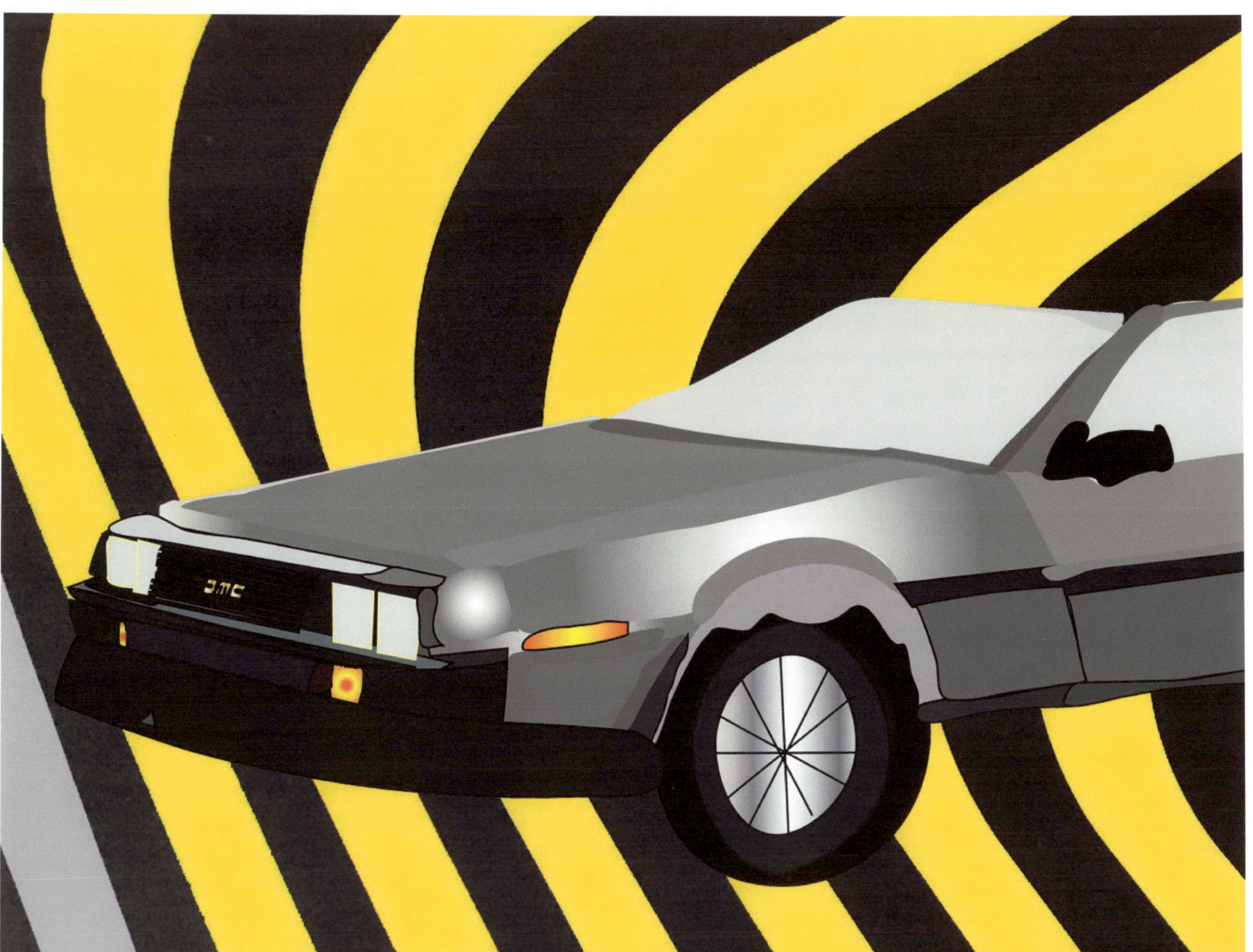

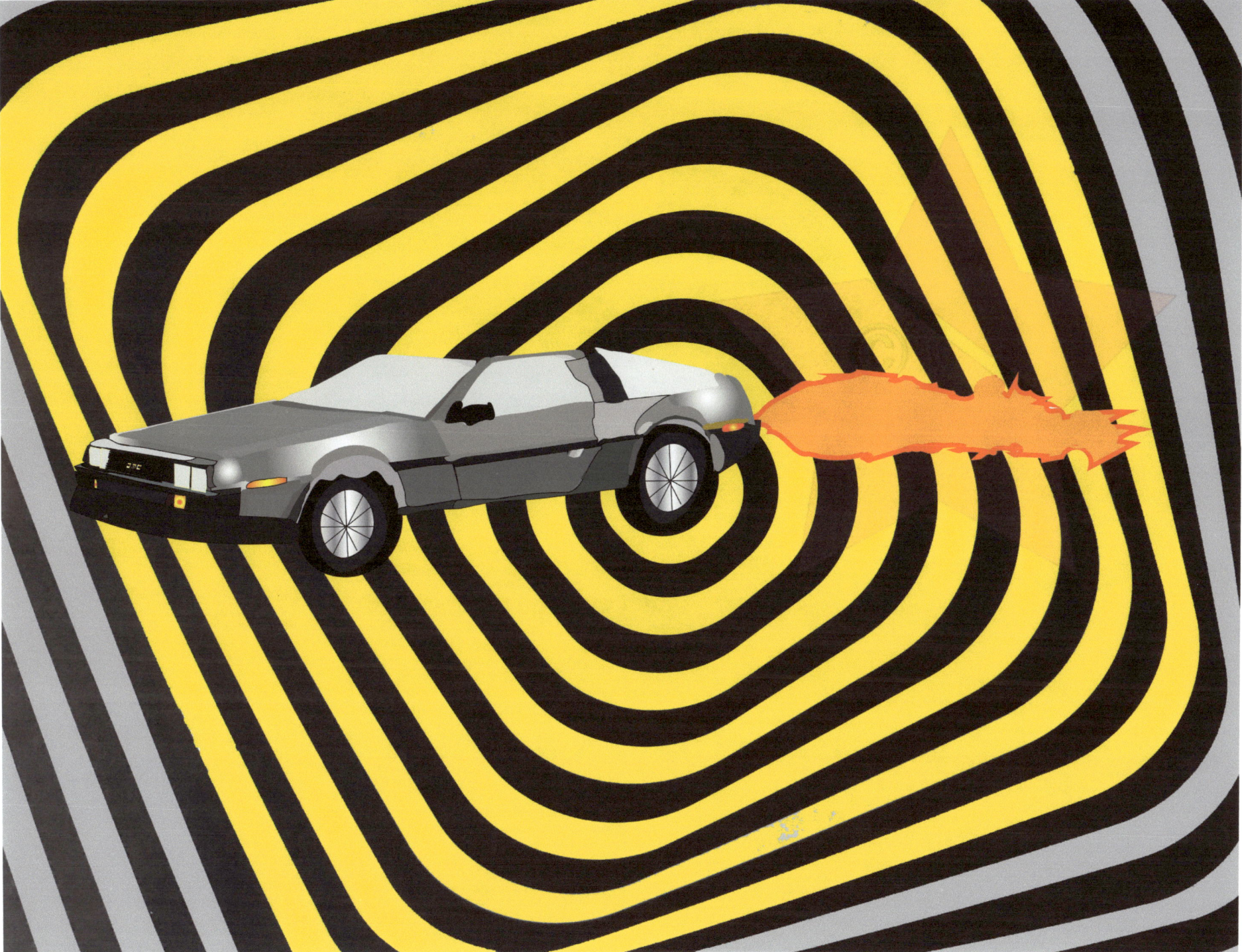

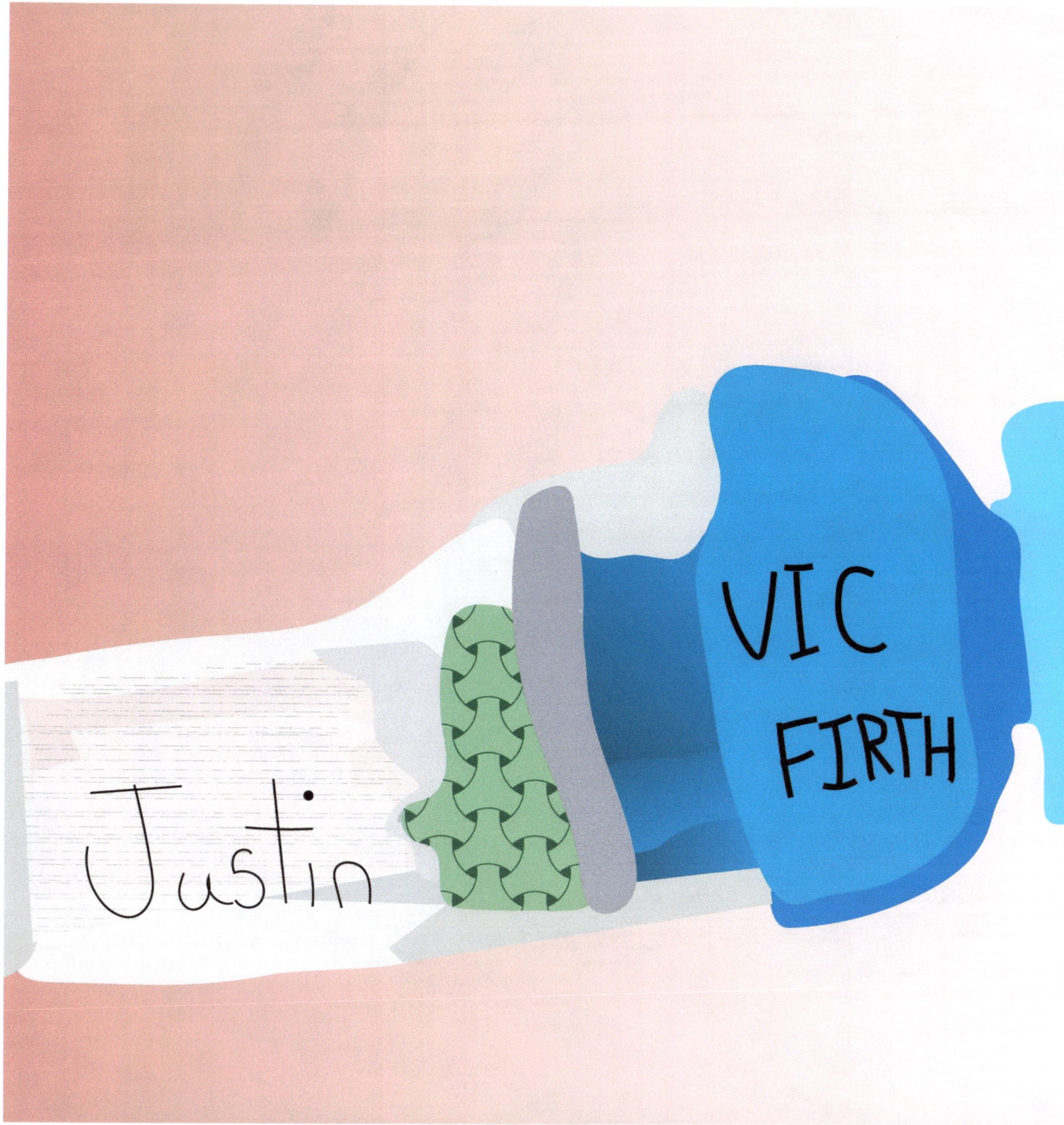
VIC
FIRTH
Justin

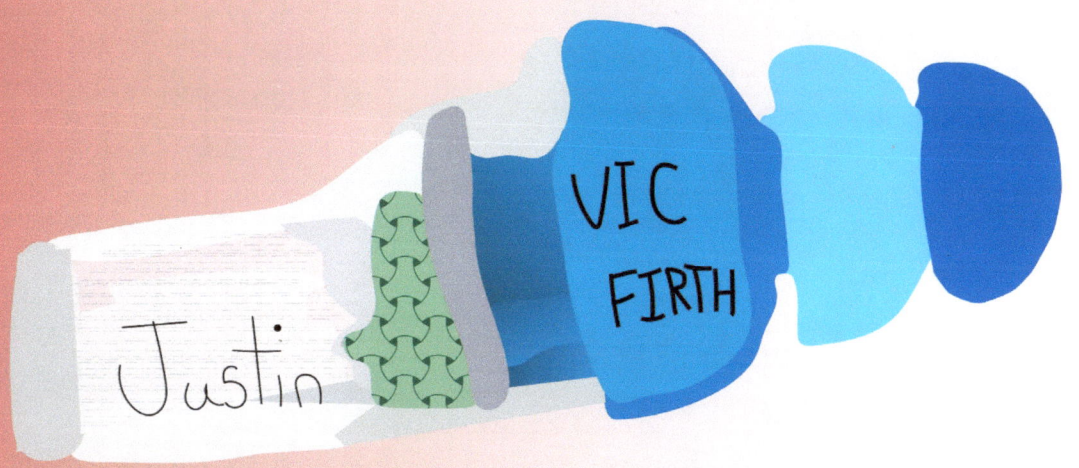

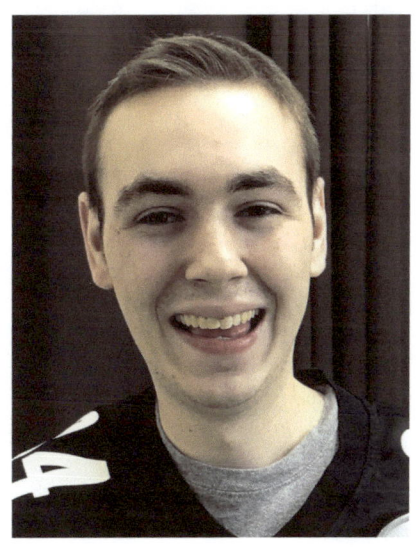

JUSTIN VALENTI
Artist on the Autism Spectrum

Justin Valenti is an artist who enjoys creating digital artwork on the computer. He has worked with this medium since middle school. Now 22 years of age, Justin works on his art at home and at a local art program in Rockville, Maryland. He is inspired by pop culture and optical illusions. In this book, Justin combines 80's pop with iconography from the past, present, and future. When he is not creating artwork, Justin enjoys reading and spending time with family and friends. Justin lives in Gaithersburg, Maryland with his family and his dog, Tom.

A special thank you to my friends, relatives, and Exceptional Minds for supporting me in everything that I achieve!